Renewing the Mind

Renewing the Mind

THE FOUNDATION OF YOUR SUCCESS

by
Casey Treat

Harrison House
Tulsa, Oklahoma

05 04   10 9 8 7 6 5 4

Renewing the Mind—
The Foundation of Your Success
ISBN 1-57794-190-X
Copyright © 1999 by Casey D. Treat
P. O. Box 98800
Seattle, Washington 98198

Published by Harrison House, Inc.
P. O. Box 35035
Tulsa, Oklahoma 74153

CONTENTS

The Christian life is the most glorious life a human being can experience, but it is not always a bed of roses. God has provided salvation from spiritual death, sin and sickness, but He did not save us from our own attitudes, choices or the problems of this world. While we can never improve upon what Jesus has done for us, we must learn how to "work out our salvation" and live it in a successful and victorious way. (Phil. 2:12.)

Have you ever wondered why many "good" Christians sin? why good Christians backslide? why good Christian marriages fail?

The reason is that without a lifestyle dedicated to the Lord, the spirit of a Christian's mind can drag him back into the behavior of the "old man," and the old pre-conversion lifestyle can take over again. So there are many thinking patterns that must be "reprogrammed" when a Christian's spirit man is born again. Paul calls this reprogramming a transformational process which takes place by the renewing of the mind. (Rom. 12:2.) In Ephesians 4:23 he says to **be renewed in the spirit of your mind.** James calls this process the "saving of our souls." (James 1:21.)

In this book I go into much detail about this process in order for you to learn the biblical principles for renewing your mind and, as a result, learn how to live the highest level of life possible in His image.

The past twenty-three years of growing a family with Wendy and growing a church of over 6,000 members has taught me that to be born again is only the first step in successful Christianity. Many never take the next steps and end up divorcing their spouse, experiencing disease or living below their destiny.

Let's go all the way to God's perfect will on earth! **You will prosper and live in health even as your soul prospers.** (3 John 2.)

I remember thinking, *Be cool, drive carefully and don't attract any attention to yourself,* as I drove south on Interstate 5 on my way home to Tacoma. I had smoked a few joints and taken some other drugs, but I knew what was going on. I also knew that if I could just stay awake, I would be home in a few minutes.

Little did I realize that even while those thoughts were going through my mind, I had gone unconscious and driven the car into the median dividing the north and south lanes. My car sat stuck deep in the mud, wheels turning at 55 miles per hour, going nowhere. God only knows how long I sat there, my tires flinging mud into the air, while I thought I was being careful not to attract any attention to myself.

The next thing I remember was the flashing of lights and a man's voice yelling at me to turn the car off. At first I wondered why he was so upset. Then I realized, *Oh, no, not again! I've blown it the "one more time" I was warned not to blow it again,* and I knew what the results would be.

It didn't take the officer long to conclude that I was loaded, and we headed for the Pierce County Jail. I had been through the routine four or five times before: pictures, prints, strip search—then into the tank. The feelings were always the same—emptiness, hurt, fear, anger and every other negative emotion imaginable. I spent that night in jail and started the process of trying to get out the next day.

Why would a nineteen-year-old kid put himself through this time and time again?

Why did I want to stay loaded twenty-four hours a day?

Why, when my life was not *that* bad, was I so willing to throw everything away?

Since I had been in jail several times already, I was given a choice this time to either go to a state penitentiary for a maximum of one year or to the Washington Drug Rehabilitation Center. I knew I didn't want prison, so I chose the drug rehabilitation center. I hid as many drugs as I could in the lining of my clothes before I left. I was nineteen years old, depressed, scared and all alone. I felt like I was old enough to die, and I was afraid that if I did die, eternity might be worse.

Not long after I entered the center, I realized the people there were different. They had a spirit of joy and freedom I hadn't seen in any "square" person before. I wanted it—I had been looking for that kind of freedom for years. So I turned in my drugs and began to learn a new lifestyle.

I soon discovered that these people were all born again and baptized with the Holy Spirit. I didn't know what that meant, but if that was what made them so happy, I wanted it. And in November of 1974 I got it—I was born again. Jesus became the Lord of my life. I was also filled with His Spirit and began to pray in other tongues. A tremendous peace, joy and liberty came into my life. I had become a Christian!

At first I thought Christians had it all together, never had a problem and lived happily ever after. But it didn't take long to realize that this wasn't the case. Many of the drug rehabilitation residents who had been saved and filled with the Spirit ended up back on the streets in worse condition than before. I saw church members still bound in fear, bitterness, depression and other problems.

After twenty-one months of residency, I became the assistant director of the center and held that position for four years. During that time, I attended a Bible college in Seattle and received a bachelor's degree in theology. When I graduated from the school and the drug rehabilitation center in January of 1980, my wife, Wendy, and I started Christian Faith Center, which I still pastor.

Since those days in the rehabilitation center—after four years of school and now twenty years of pastoring—I have gained a much greater understanding of why so many Christians never walk in the peace, joy and freedom of their salvation. So many try to break free from the hold of the world and its hurts, but they never succeed. It isn't that they haven't been truly born again or that they didn't really believe. For these struggling believers, the problem isn't in their spirits; it's in their souls. Their minds haven't been renewed. Though their spirits have been recreated, their minds are still old.

If you are like most in the church today, you're thinking that there is more to God's plan for your life but you're not sure how to get to it; take hope. There is more.

You have been predestined to be conformed to the image of Jesus, and you will get there. You will experience change as your mind is renewed to God's Word. You can walk in the freedom of God's blessed, abundant life through the renewing of your mind. If you will take the time to allow the Holy Spirit to work with you as you read through the following pages, I believe you will grow spiritually, mentally, physically, financially and socially.

As you study and work through the truth in the chapters that follow, don't just look for interesting information. Examine those areas of your life that have been difficult, limiting or negative, and see how you can begin to change the spirit of your mind in those areas. The many renewal steps and questions you will find in every chapter have been provided to assist you in this process so you can experience God's very best in every area of life.

I have provided the steps to personal transformation following many of the chapters to help you record and work through the crucial process of spiritual mind renewal. After each chapter studied, please plan to answer the questions and review the chapter material as a time of reflection.

Decide within yourself today to receive God's truth that will set you free into the joy of the Spirit's new birth!

"And you shall know the truth, and the truth shall make you free."

John 8:32

—Pastor Casey Treat

1

THE GREATEST DAY OF MY LIFE

The greatest day of my life was September of 1974, and I found myself sitting in the hallway of the Washington Drug Rehabilitation Center. I was in shock because I had just been given a choice by the county judge to either go to prison for a minimum of a year or enter rehabilitation for at least two years. As I sat there, I thought, *I'm really not that bad. I've just had a few unlucky breaks that keep landing me in jail. It isn't my fault. It's the police or the school administration or society or something, but not me. Just ask my mom, and she'll tell you; it's the crowd I hang out with.*

But reality began to sink in as I went through a very difficult interview and was finally accepted into the program. While I was scared, mad and embarrassed that I needed to be put away to get my head together, I was also excited and desired a new life. By nineteen, I had ruined my health both physically and mentally, filled several file folders with various reports at the county jail and alienated my family and friends. Though I denied it on the inside, I really wanted to change; but how could I?

Somehow I had bought into the concept that you are what you are and there's nothing you can do about it. I was doing a miserable job of living my natural, physical life, and I certainly had no idea of the abundant spiritual life God had made available to me through the Cross of Jesus Christ. But I soon learned that I could change and make my life into whatever I wanted it to be. It wouldn't be an instantaneous experience, but with God's help it would be a miraculous one, full of abundance and excitement.

As my life began to be reshaped, rebuilt and renewed, I found I had a destiny in God that involved a rewarding lifestyle with a purpose. I also found out that most people are like I was in that they don't like some part of their lives but feel unable to do anything about it.

Today, twenty-five years after that day I sat in the rehab center, I spend all of my time with those I pastor and minister to daily, sharing the wonderful blessing of God's abundant life. And there has never been a more crucial time for the Church to grow up into its fullness. In the late fifties, sixties and seventies God began to remind the Church about the importance of faith. It was also during this time that the Charismatic message hit many traditional churches, and large independent congregations like ours in Seattle began to spring up.

God was saying, "You've got to walk by faith, you've got to be filled with the Spirit and you've got to pray with the Spirit." He was bringing us revelation upon revelation, insight upon insight, line upon line from the Word of God to stop us from being a bunch of traditional, religious people. Jesus died and rose from the dead to birth a people who could live at God's level of spiritual life—people who wouldn't feel at home in the world. So He reintroduced His Word and ways to us during those years to inspire us to become the Church He wants us to be.

But we will not live the life Jesus died to give us if we hold on to old, traditional, carnal or negative ways of thinking. Even though it's a new millennium, we've still got a long way to go.

It's time to make some changes in the body of Christ today, because very few of us are experiencing the abundant life which God sent His Spirit and Word in order to give us. So in this book, we will examine those biblical processes of change that allow God's purpose and Spirit to dominate our lives and bring us to His perfect plan for our lives.

ABUNDANT LIFE

Every believer is called to live a life that is abundant, increasing and always expanding. Words like *growing, improving, expanding* and *increasing* are the vocabulary of God's abundant life. Abundant life is about always moving forward and rising higher. When life on earth started in Genesis 1, the Spirit of the Lord started moving across the earth, and He has never stopped since then.

Jesus said, **"And these signs will follow those who believe"** (Mark 16:17).

The abundant life of God is a life that grows and moves forward every day. Jesus says in John 10:10 that the devil, the thief, comes to steal, kill and destroy. He wants to keep you from living. He wants to rob from your life. Everything that's negative, everything that removes, everything that stops and kills is of the thief, the devil.

But Jesus said, "I have come that you may have life and that you may have it more abundantly." Oh, I love that thought! So in our first look at God's spiritual process of victorious transformation, I want to put God's thoughts of abundance in your mind. I want to inspire you with His thoughts of increase and thoughts of moving forward and upward.

These thoughts may not be normal to many of you. I know this because we live in a world in which many people are trying just to survive. Many of you reading are just trying to make a living and trying to make it through to the end.

So many in the Church today have lowered their vision and are trying just to hang on until Jesus comes. So many are trying just to survive and are moping and hoping the Antichrist won't put the mark of the beast on them. Many Christians are so defeated that they wish Jesus would come back tonight. They have no vision for tomorrow, and they're like prisoners, waiting for an escape.

This is not the abundant life of God; it is the life of religion and the expectation of tradition. This is the attitude of people who don't know the life that God has called them to. So many "pew warming" Christians have been raised so long in the religious culture of just making a living and trying to hang in there that they don't know God's abundance even exists. The negative, sick, sorrowful environment they were raised in keeps them constantly confused. They're always wondering what's happening. Their lives are not what God willed. Their vision is not what God planned. What they see for tomorrow is not what God sees for tomorrow.

What God sees for tomorrow is what He sees every day: exciting, progressing, abundant life. Jesus said, **"I have come that they may have life, and that they may have it more abundantly"** (John 10:10).

So let's look at God's gift of abundant life that Jesus came to offer, because everything that follows in these pages is intended to help you realize the truth of this gift.

The Greek word for life spoken by Jesus in John 10:10 is *zoe*.[1] It means "absolute life, the purest kind of life, life in its very essence." I like what the margin note in my Bible reads: "the God kind of life."

Jesus didn't say, "I've come for you to *exist*." You can exist without Jesus. He didn't say, "I've come for you to *survive*." You can survive without Jesus. He didn't say, "I've come for you to *make a living*." You can make a living without Jesus. No, Jesus said, "I've come that you might have the God kind of *absolute life, the purest kind of life, life in its very essence—zoe*."

Anything that's alive on God's green planet is growing. Because God created it, anything that's living will get bigger and better. Every living thing in His magnificent creation blossoms and reproduces after its own kind. (Gen. 1:11,12.) So the very essence of God is life.

Theologically, we debate the essence of God. You know, theologians sit around in their cemeteries—uh, excuse me, I mean *seminaries*—and discuss the deep things of theology that mean absolutely nothing! But for the sake of proving how smart I am, humor me, and let's discuss God's theological essence just a little bit.

THE ESSENCE OF GOD

When raising the subject for discussion, some theologians would say the essence of God is righteousness. Righteousness, or justice, is at the heart of God. "There's nothing but justice," some would say. Others would say, "It's holiness—everything emanates out of the core of holiness." Still others would say, "Love is at the very core of God's being."

None of these are bad. But I'm telling you, you can't have righteousness or holiness or love if you're not alive. And you can't love anyone if you're not alive. So the true essence of God is life. The Bible says God is life. **"I have set before you life.... For He is your life."** (Deut. 30:19,20.) The very heart of God's being is pure, absolute life! That's why when people touched Jesus' cloak, everyone who was sick got healed.

Think about this. Grab some of God's thoughts. Take a new look at John 10:10 now. When Jesus said, "I've come that you might have life," He was saying, "I have come to give you God's being—His essence." Jesus came to put the essence of God's being into your being. He came to give you *zoe* in every area of life. God wants to walk and talk in your home through you as you raise your kids. He wants to put His life in that checking account and in those finances. He wants to walk and talk through you in your marriage and on the job, because God came that you might have life!

God came to give you life, not some kind of survival existence. You don't have to mope around, just hanging on.

So to make sure we understand: Jesus said, He brings life more abundantly. *Whoo!* That's the way He is. *More abundantly!* Everything God does is big, good and abundant. He didn't create some small, ugly little planet and put you on it. He created a gigantic, abundant earth and said, "Welcome to earth, Adam. This is where you're going to live and take dominion. Think big."

God doesn't give His born-again children some narrow, little destiny and survival mentality. He called us to a glorious life of abundance. When Jesus goes fishing, it's a net-breaking, boat-sinking load of fish! (John 21: 4-6.) When Jesus holds a luncheon, He feeds 5,000 people with two fish and five loaves and twelve baskets left over. (John 6:7-13.) So where did we get this small-living mentality? Where did we get this competitive, jealous, poverty-stricken mind-set? From sick and tired folks who are sick and tired.

It's so sad to see born-again Christians who are just about to give up, but trying to hang in there and meagerly survive till the end. It's time to start living the abundant life. The Greek word for *abundance* is "perissos,"[2] and it carries with it the sense of being beyond. It means "superabundant in quantity and superior in quality." Oh, I like that! Do we want the best? Do we want the most? I do. I want the best quality of life God has to offer!

God didn't tell us to take either abundance or just enough. He called us to have abundance, which also means by implication *excessive*. Now, excessive is a tough word for some because they were raised by sweet little ol' parents who lived through the Depression. So their attitude is to cut back, save, hold on to what they have and be careful.

So many Christians have that spirit. They have a conservative mind-set. I'm not talking politically; I'm talking about the way they view life. They have been programmed from early in life to have a this-is-good-enough mentality that sees excess as evil and wrong. But I'm telling you right now, if this bunch doesn't get their minds renewed in this life, they're going to get a headache in heaven!

The reason we think those kinds of thoughts—thoughts which tell us, *This is enough. This is good enough. Excess is wrong. Abundance is bad*—is that the only thing on our minds is ourselves.

When someone says, "This little bit is enough for me," that's fine, as long as he's the only person on his mind. But God didn't call us to live for ourselves. God didn't say, "You are the center of this universe, so just stay focused on yourself." That is selfish thinking.

Some time ago a person came to me and said, "Pastor Treat, I don't agree with your preaching on prosperity." So I said, "Well, first of all, it's not mine. I'm just reading it out of the Bible." But I was curious, so I asked, "Why don't you agree?"

"Well, I'm living a good life," he answered. "All my needs are met, and I'm happy just the way I am. I don't need any more."

I said, "That's fine if you're the only person on this planet. But what are you doing for hungry people in South America? How are you going to help the suffering, struggling Church in China? And what was the last thing you did for sighing, crying, dying people in the Middle East who don't know Jesus? I'm glad that all your needs are met, but when are you going to think about someone else's needs?"

I want people in my church to prosper so they can help the Bulgarians we visit every year who are believing God for heat! I want the congregation I serve at Christian Faith Center to understand and live in God's abundant life so they can go over and touch a billion Chinese who don't have the car, the home, the kitchen or even the closet our church members have.

We need to get off this, "I'm doing okay, so let everybody else go jump" mentality and get a hold of the life Jesus died to provide! Abundant life! We're not the only people on this planet. We're called to go out there and spread this thing around and make a difference in our world. God is counting on us to show the world's people His love and goodness.

Having the God kind of life—that which is superabundant in quantity, superior in quality, in effect excess—is what life is all about. I want to live an extreme life: I want to have an extremely good marriage.

I want to have extremely good times with my family. I want to have extremely happy kids. I want to have an extremely good church. I want to have an extremely effective ministry. I want those in my church to have extremely prosperous businesses. This is what our extreme God is all about.

If you barely have enough resources to pay your own kids' tuition, how are you going to reach the kids of this earth? If you barely have enough gas to get yourself to church, how are you going to fund traveling expenses for the missionaries of this world? If you're struggling to believe God to pay your bills, how are you going to pay the bills for ministries all over the planet?

Come on! Get out of your barely-get-by, self-centered world! Come on into God's great big world, where life is good, and it's more abundant.

ABUNDANT IN FINANCES

Second Corinthians 8:9 says Jesus became poor to make His Church rich:

> **For you know the grace of our Lord Jesus Christ, that though He was rich, yet for your sakes He became poor, that you through His poverty might become rich.**

The Amplified Bible says:

> **For you are becoming progressively acquainted with and recognizing more strongly and clearly the grace of our Lord Jesus Christ (His kindness, His gracious generosity, His undeserved favor and spiritual blessing), [in] that though He was [so very] rich, yet for your sakes He became [so very] poor, in order that by His poverty you might become enriched (abundantly supplied).**

There's that phrase again—*abundantly supplied.* And for those who get nervous about taking Scripture out of context, read chapters 8 and 9 of Paul's second letter to the Corinthian church, and you'll see there is no question that the context is finances.

Yes, thank God that He brings abundance in the spiritual realm—that's the traditional interpretation of this verse. Yes, He brings abundance in the soul realm. But 2 Corinthians 8:9 says He became poor so you could also have abundance in the financial realm. He even goes so far as to say that through His poverty you might be *rich*.

God sent His Son, and He became poor so you could become rich. So don't tell me you're "poor for the Lord." You have it backwards: He became poor for you. Don't think that your lack or your poverty is glorifying God. No, it's when we prosper financially in abundant life that God is glorified. God gets no glory when we walk around with a religious image of God. There is no glory in being whipped, sick, poor, sad and in despair. This doesn't show the world what Jesus did for them.

I know I'm kicking some sacred cows and religious tradition. But I'm only teaching what's in God's Word.

Let's look at some more of what Paul had to say about God's abundance in Philippians 4:19:

My God shall supply all your need *according* to His riches in glory by Christ Jesus.

Paul is telling us here that God will supply everything we as His Church need to live an abundant life, everything we need to fulfill His will, everything we need to fulfill our destinies.

God doesn't fulfill our needs according to the condition of the stock market. It's not according to what your boss wants to pay you. It's not according to the contracts your union fought for. It's not according to your company's profits. It's according to *His* riches in glory. You may want to trust in the Dow Jones industrial average or in the Teamsters or in your boss and company. But I'm going to trust God. He is the

One who promises to meet all my need and yours according to His *riches* in glory.

The Amplified Bible says, **My God will liberally supply (fill to the full) your every need according to His riches in glory in Christ Jesus.** You won't find any of this "barely enough" stuff in Scripture. What you will find is phrases like, *liberally supply...fill to the full...according to His riches.* If Paul were just talking about what we need to survive—air, water, food and shelter, we wouldn't need to call on His riches in glory. But Paul is talking abundant-life talk. He's talking about God's giving you what you need to live this abundant life so you can fulfill your destiny. And to do this, the apostle says that God will use His riches in glory to make sure you have a liberal supply.

Now please understand: This book isn't just another prosperity message book. God hasn't called me to write prosperity message books. God has called me to write on the subject of mind renewal and spiritual change. But if you can't even see His will in natural things, you will never realize His will in spiritual things.

Many Christians think of church as small, poor, kind of silly and certainly not cool, certainly not current and certainly not abundant. So I want to challenge your thinking about church. One of the most common comments we get from people visiting Christian Faith Center is that it's so big. They say that because they think of a church as a little white building with a steeple and a little bell in it, you know.

It's okay for our local Seattle Seahawks football stadium to have sixty-thousand seats.

It's okay for the Seattle Mariners baseball park to have fifty-thousand seats.

It's okay for rock-and-roll concert auditoriums to have twenty-thousand seats.

But for church, the image most have of us is just a little group. We've got Sister Beulah on the organ and Brother Sam leading praise and worship with about thirty to eighty adults. And when we reach into our pockets, moths fly out. So as a first step in mind renewal, the Church today must develop a new mentality about church.

The church in Jerusalem had 50,000 members when the apostles began to spread out! The church in Antioch had approximately 35,000 members when they sent Paul out on his first missionary journey. This wasn't a ragtag band of barely-hanging-in-there Christians hiding out in a little white building. This wasn't a bunch of unimportant religious people hiding from the devil. No, this was a church full of Christians whose attitude was, *We're going to turn the world upside down!*

This was the church Paul talked about in Ephesians 5:25-33 when he used the analogy of marriage and the Church.

> **Husbands, love your wives, just as Christ also loved the church and gave Himself for it, that He might sanctify and cleanse it with the washing of water by the word, that He might present it to Himself a glorious church, not having spot or wrinkle or any such thing, but that it should be holy and without blemish. So husbands ought to love their own wives as their own bodies; he who loves his wife loves himself. For no one ever hated his own flesh, but nourishes and cherishes it, just as the Lord does the church. For we are members of His body, of His flesh and of His bones. "For this reason a man shall leave his father and mother and be joined to his wife, and the two shall become one flesh." This is a great mystery, but I speak concerning Christ and the church.**
>
> **Nevertheless let each one of you in particular so love his own wife as himself, and let the wife see that she respects her husband.**

This passage really isn't about marriage, although we use it to teach about that. It talks about the Church and Jesus. We know this because says this in verse 32: "I'm speaking about the Church and Jesus." So he teaches, "Husbands, love your wives as Christ loved the Church and gave Himself for it."

When Jesus offered Himself for the sins of the world, He gave the Church everything heaven had to offer. He gave us His grace, the Holy Spirit and God's richest blessings. Why? Verse 26 tells us why: **That He might sanctify and cleanse it with the washing of water by the word.**

Jesus gave the Church the best heaven had to offer to clean us up and straighten us up! We get clean by the Word! We get sanctified by the Word! We get better by the Word! We get stronger by the Word! We get bigger by the Word! But it can't and won't happen unless we renew our minds ourselves with the Word.

You don't need guilt, abuse, poverty, lack or sickness to be cleansed. You don't need religious retribution to be cleansed. "Well, the Lord gave me this cancer to try to clean up my life" someone might say. No, that doesn't clean up your life. In fact, it will kill you if you don't know God's healing power. The Word sanctifies the Church so **that He might present it to Himself a glorious church.**

Now this brings another word into our discussion—*glory*. The word *glory* implies "the presence of God." A Greek dictionary says *glory* "carries the connotation of His dignity, His blessing and the manifestation of His will."[3] It is the Greek word *doxa,* and it literally means splendor, brightness, dignity, kingly honor.[4]

God meets all our life needs according to His riches in glory by Christ Jesus. God uses His glory to help us live. This is the same word Paul uses in 2 Corinthians 3:18 when he says we are changed from glory to glory. This is God's plan for the Church. We are to be a glorious, bright, splendid Church, not having spot or wrinkle or any blemish, and full of God's superabundant life. We should be shaking our fists at the devil and making him run, not the other way around.

Now somebody may say, "Well, all that's going to happen when we get to heaven." But they're wrong, because it's got to happen *before* we get there. That's when we get presented to Jesus—when we get to heaven. So before we can be presented, we've got to become glorious, spotless, without wrinkles.

We can't be a bunch of poverty-stricken, sick and barely-hanging-in-there vagabonds staggering into heaven, complaining, "Thank God we got off that planet! Man, the devil was beating us up and down! We're so sick, and we're so poor. Thank God we don't have to go through that anymore!" No! That's not how it's going to be when we go to heaven.

WELCOME HOME, TROOPS!

When we get to heaven we will be a glorious Church, living an abundant life. All our needs will have been supplied according to His riches in glory. We will have victoriously fulfilled our mission on earth. Our going to heaven will be a victory march. It will be a sight that eclipses the sight of American troops coming home from World War II. We will be marching home after destroying the enemy, not the other way around.

But until we become like that, we aren't going anywhere—we're too wrinkly and spotted.

Somebody might say, "The Lord's coming back tonight." Okay, but if that's true, you must be glorious, because that's what He's coming back to receive. Are you glorious? Are you an example of abundant life? Are you everything that God wants you to be? Or is your idea of the Lord's return some kind of rescue, because you've never come up to the place of life that He planned for you?

READY OR NOT, HERE WE (DON'T) COME!

I understand the trials we all go through with this. I go through the same thing. We all want to believe what we heard on a Christian TV show—that He's coming back tonight. If He comes back tonight, we don't have to make any more car payments, and we don't have to pay off our credit cards.

"Hallelujah! Free, free at last!" we say. No more mortgage payments. No more worries about putting our kids through college. No more spiritual preparation. No more faith building. No more being honest business people. No more renewing our minds and developing our character—because we get to escape! We get to get out of here and go to heaven! Hey, hey, hey!

And while we're waiting to go to heaven, you hear some say, "I just pray that I might hold on until the end, because it's all going to be okay on the other side." We sing a popular song, "When we all get to heaven, what a day of rejoicing that will be. When we all see Jesus, we'll sing and shout the victory."[5] The message of that popular church song sounds good, but what it really means is, "Until then, we have no victory and just a little bit of rejoicing. We're just a sad bunch."

So many of us have been raised to believe that sort of beggarly nonsense. But that's not the Bible! He's not coming back for that kind of Church. He's coming back for a victorious Church. And by the way, the Bible says we are to test, or judge, all things. (1 Thess. 5:21.) So when you hear someone saying, "The Lord's coming back real soon," examine what they're saying, and you'll notice it's usually tied with, "Buy my book or send an offering to my ministry, because the Lord's coming back. We don't have much time. So let me give you my book on the beginning of the end, the last days and the ramifications of the mark of the beast."

Come on, we want to be childlike, but we don't want to be a bunch of childish guppies. Check it out. Use some spiritual sense. That same guy who said Jesus is coming back this year is building a new building with your donation! And the book he sent you as a partner gift for your donation says the Lord's coming back this year. So something's up!

I heard with my own little, ol' ears one of these last-days types say, "This could be the last year that you'll be able to give into this missionary outreach. So if you'll send your offering now, we'll be ready for the coming of the Lord by the end of this year." This same group is out buying new television stations! What are they doing all that for? I mean, if their predictions are true, those stations won't even be on the air until next year! And if the Lord's coming back *this year,* what are they going to do with the stations they're building with that Second Coming money you gave them that won't even be on the air until next year? I'd say there is something rotten in Denmark with this deal!

In the Lord's prayer Jesus did not teach us to pray, "Thy kingdom, I'm coming…" He said to pray, **Thy kingdom *come*. Thy will be done *in earth*** (Matt. 6:10 KJV). We are not called to escape from the earth; we are called to establish God's will and God's kingdom on earth: **...that we may have great boldness in the day of judgment because *as He is so are we in this world*** (1 John 4:17).

Yes, we believe the Lord is coming back, but we've got to wake up. He's not coming back for a poor, sick Church who is waiting to escape the world's mess. No! He's coming back for a *glorious* Church. So we have a ways to go, and I wouldn't worry about His return very soon.

Before Jesus returns we're going to have to get our minds off ourselves and on that world out there. We're going to have to rise to a new level of life—God's kind of life.

Before Jesus returns, His Church must rise to the place in God's abundant life where we are spending more time getting other folks healed than we are trying to get healed ourselves.

Before Jesus returns, the Church must rise to the level of spending more time giving to the poor than being poor ourselves.

Before Jesus returns, the Church must rise to God's abundant level of life, at which point, our needs are met according to His riches in glory and we are the glorious Church Ephesians 5 talks about. When we are shining in His glory, the world will look at us and say, "How do you do it? How do you have that kind of marriage? How do you raise those kinds of kids? How do you live that kind of life?"

So we will tell them, "You've got to get in the glorious Church."

"Well, what kind of church is that?" they will ask. "I thought churches sang old songs. I thought preachers just got up there and talked a bunch of rubbish that didn't make a difference in everyday life. I thought you just needed a crutch to make it through life while you waited for Jesus to rescue you off the planet!"

"Well, you were wrong," we will say. "We're changing the planet, not escaping anything. The devil's hoping *he* can get raptured, because we're beating the hell out of him! We aren't leaving! The earth was given to the saints! And WE AREN'T LEAVING until we possess it! WE AREN'T LEAVING until we subdue this planet. WE AREN'T LEAVING until we take dominion over this planet!"

Abundant life will rally the Church toward battle, not away from it. We're not to be like Jonah, trying to run out of town and get away from Nineveh, the city God sent him to. No, we're called to march right into the middle of Nineveh, with signs and wonders following the preaching of the glorious, abundant message Jesus died to bring.

The Church is called to take dominion over the devil's works in Jesus' name. And we can and will do this as we allow our minds to be changed. So that is what this book is about: spiritual change, the kind that makes us shine as glorious lights of God's reflection in the world.

In the next chapter we will look at the glory of God's image and see how a healthy view of who He is affects our own image of ourselves.

2

THE IMAGE OF GOD

The will of God for man is clear from Genesis to Revelation: Possess this planet. In essence God said, "You, Adam and Eve, take dominion." (Gen. 1:26-28.) "You, My Church, preach the gospel to every ethnic group so that those who follow My teaching and humble themselves before Me will inherit the earth." (Matt. 28:19,20.) We were created in the likeness and image of God (Gen.1:26), and the Lord has called us to live that way—with authority and dominion. He wants us to be like His Son, because we are sons and daughters, and walk in His image.

Never once in Scripture is the Church ever told to escape the world. We are never told to run away from it. Nor are we told to be defeated and hide in fear, just hoping that we can get out of here. No, we were told to be a glorious Church.

As I have stated, a glorious Church is one that's living in the presence of God, where the dignity, blessing and will of God are seen by everyone who looks. And this is the kind of person God wants you to be—a glorious person in the midst of a glorious, victorious Church. Once the Church is glorious, then and only then will Jesus return to present us spotless to the Father. So I'm personally very unconcerned about all the "imminent return" hype these last-days-Rapture-eschatology teachers have been preaching lately, because we've got a long way to go and a lot of work to do. I realize the Lord can do a quick work in these last days, but I believe He wants us focused on fulfilling His will, not trying to avoid His will and let millions go to hell while we go to heaven.

Now if all we had to do to take on God's image was be born again, Jesus would have probably returned for the Church yesterday. But becoming glorious is a transformational process that happens after we are born again. Paul says we can see the process as we begin renewing our minds until we take on the image of the Lord: **We all, with unveiled face, beholding as in a mirror the glory of the Lord, are being transformed into the same image from glory to glory, just as by the Spirit of the Lord** (2 Cor. 3:18).

When you were being raised by your family, you subconsciously took on the physical image and mannerisms of whoever raised you. Subconsciously you took on their attitudes and beliefs as well. Whether it was your parents, your grandparents or whomever, you didn't really try to take on their image. It just naturally happened when you grew up under them. If you were raised in the North, you talk and think differently than folks raised in the American South. If you were raised in Europe, you have a completely distinct image and language that developed through living there. And that's your image.

If you were to see my son's walk, you would say, "He walks just like Casey." And he does, although he didn't try to do that. He was just raised in my image.

Now some of the image you take on from your parents can, of course, be good. But the ungodly image and presence many grow up under can hold them down and keep them from the abundant life of Christ even after they're born again. Unless transformation takes place, they may stagger into heaven, but they will experience very little victory in this life as members of the Church.

So we are going to focus on the importance of renewing our image in accordance with God's image. But before we can do that, we have to understand the true image of God, because when you have a false image of God, it corrupts your image of abundant life.

Every culture and religion that has unwittingly followed Satan's plan of personal destruction has brought into it the false image he has peddled about God. If a culture or religion teaches that God is, say, a tree or that He just doesn't care, that's going to affect how a person lives. So let's look at what the Bible has to say about some of the enemy's deceptions. Then we will look at the true image of God and see how that same glorious image has been imparted to His Church.

In Romans 1:20 Paul says:

> **For since the creation of the world His invisible attributes are clearly seen, being understood by the things that are made, even His eternal power and Godhead, so that they are without excuse.**

Now all Paul means here is that even if you've never darkened the door of a Christian church, you can look around at what God made and know a lot about Him. You can see that He's big, He's beautiful, He loves variety, He loves change, He loves openness, He loves balance. You only need to be alive on our planet, Paul says, to visibly know that there is a God.

You can learn a lot about God just by looking at His artwork. The same is true of human artists. For example, when you look at Picasso's art, you learn about him. Poor guy. That guy's brain was a mess, and you can see it in his art. But when you look at God's art that surrounds us, you can see the creative majesty of His Godhead in such a physical way that Paul says it should drive men to their knees.

Nevertheless, Paul goes on to say in verse 21 that many don't care:

> **...because, although they knew God, they did not glorify Him as God, nor were thankful, but became futile in their thoughts, and their foolish hearts were darkened.**

You see, here's the wrong image problem! It all has to do with what you do with your thoughts. Paul tells us here how the world walked away from God because they became confused and negative. And we have seen this happen in every generation over and over since Paul wrote this. God inspires a revival; He is revealed to the world, but then the process of futile, foolish thinking starts over again.

So as we read through Romans 1:20-21, we can see how corrupting God's image lures people away from what God has for them. And it all starts with thoughts. How you perceive God in your thoughts determines everything else in your life.

Proverbs 23:7 says, **As [a man] thinks in his heart, so is he.** The kind of people Paul is writing about in Romans 1:22-23 **became fools, and changed the glory of the incorruptible God into an image made like corruptible man—and birds and four-footed beasts, and creeping things.** They changed the glory of God into something made by man because of the corrupted thoughts in their hearts. And men still do it.

So we must always be careful to guard our hearts. The thoughts you think will either lighten or darken your heart. If your thoughts are full of God's thoughts, your heart will be light. But if your thoughts are dark, your heart will be dark.

Listen to some of the darkened thoughts of our present generation: *Hey! We don't believe in God, but we'll die to save the whale. We'll pay you to kill the human baby, but we'll put you in jail if you kill an eagle's baby!* Men have always changed what's important and perverted it. So the glory of God is diminished.

I like how *The Message Bible* expands on Paul's message in this passage of Romans. It says:

> **People knew God perfectly well, but when they didn't treat him like God, refusing to worship him, they trivialized themselves into silliness and confusion so that there was neither sense nor direction left in their lives.**

This really describes our current world society, doesn't it? Today in America, we have trivialized ourselves into silliness and confusion. What in reality should be seen as important to us is seen as stupid, and what should be rejected as foolish and stupid is seen as important. Society makes it important because of wrong thoughts! Generation after generation of man trivializes himself into confusion so that, as this verse says, there is neither sense nor direction left in life.

The Message Bible goes on to say:

> **They pretended to know it all, but were illiterate regarding life. They traded the glory of God who holds the whole world in his hands for cheap figurines you can buy at any roadside stand...they traded the true God for a fake god, and worshiped the god they made instead of the God who made them.**

What a strong description of how people throughout history have continually recreated God into their own pathetic images! My own interpretation of this historic image problem is this: They traded the true God for a fake god and worshiped the god they made instead of the God who made them. They traded the glory of God for a cheap, 1-900 psychic phone call. They traded the glory of God for folklore and superstition.

But this also happens in the Church. About the Church you could say, "They traded the glory of God for American-made Christianity that says, 'I like my religion as long as it's comfortable and easy and doesn't cost me anything.'" In America today we want the Bible to say what we want it to say instead of what God has already said. And the results, as proven historically, have been tragic.

The Message Bible continues:

> **Worse followed. Refusing to know God, they soon didn't know how to be human either—women didn't know how to be women, men didn't know how to be men. Sexually confused, they abused and defiled one another, women with women, men with men—all lust, no love. And then they paid for it, oh, how they paid for it— emptied of God and love, godless and loveless wretches.**

Since they didn't bother to acknowledge God, God quit bothering them and let them run loose. And then all hell broke loose: rampant evil, grabbing and grasping, vicious backstabbing. They made life hell on earth with their envy, wanton killing, bickering, and cheating. Look at them: mean-spirited, venomous, fork-tongued God-bashers. Bullies, swaggerers, insufferable windbags! They keep inventing new ways of wrecking lives. They ditch their parents when they get in the way. Stupid, slimy, cruel, coldblooded. And it's not as if they don't know better. They know perfectly well they're spitting in God's face. And they don't care—worse, they hand out prizes to those who do the worst things best!

Romans 1:24-32

What a graphic description. This is what happens when sinful man creates God in his own image. The end result is that God leaves you to your own image and you die in your lust—confused and without direction. The Church must teach God's reality. But before we can do that accurately, we must get the true image of who we are in Him and who He is in us. We've got to know first that abundant life is available. Then we've got to stop our selfish ways of thinking that major on survival and what we want. We must start living bigger in such a way that we change the world around us.

When the Church understands the goodness and purpose of God, every one of us has the ability to have a home network—what we call home Bible fellowship groups at Christian Faith Center—where people can be loved, healed, saved and filled with the Spirit before going back to their families. Then they will bring others after they share the good news: "Hey! I've met a friend, and he changed my life. He acts like Jesus."

The Church who understands the goodness and purpose of God also has the ability to invest in missions and go on mission trips that touch the nations of this world. But we will never do it until we see ourselves with a new image, created in the likeness of Christ.

Without a right image of God, men worship gods of their own making to serve their selfish needs. And the outcome is a life of futility and death. This is why the first two of the Ten Commandments are:

> **"You shall have no other gods before Me. You shall not make for yourself any carved image, or any likeness of anything that is in heaven above, or that is in the earth beneath, or that is in the water under the earth."**

> Exodus 20:3-4

We think of these commandments in terms of statues, or "gods," used in idol worship. And that's partially true. But there is a bigger picture than that. God is saying to us, "Don't you make your own image of who I am. Keep a clear picture, a true image, of who I am in your life, because if you get a wrong image of who I am, you will create all kinds of problems in your life."

As we have seen in Romans 1, when people have the wrong image of God, they become like that image. If you were raised by parents who believe God kills people through the tragedy of disease or accidents to "take them home," you will see God as a to-be-feared murderer. Every time you hear of an accident or the word *cancer,* your image of God will pop up in your head.

I guarantee you will have problems when the attitudes of your parents or pastor influence you to believe that the Lord puts families in car wrecks to draw them closer together. If your God is a God of tragedy, you won't know a thing about His protection. And if you believe God puts sickness and disease on people, you won't believe in a God of healing.

You will really have problems if you believe God will allow any of these bad things to happen to you if your skirt's too far above your knees, your blouse is too low cut or if your hair is either too long or too short. Makeup is still an issue many churches think God gets angry over. Visit some of their services, and you will hear them say, "God has a measuring stick, and He's checking your skirt and hair. And if you've worn makeup this week, God is very upset." Of course, no woman would wear it there in the service. So the message is that if you've "sinned" between then and last service, you'd better look out for God.

GOD ISN'T UGLY OR MEAN

Churches who don't believe in makeup and so forth must believe God only accepts ugly people and that He's angry with those who don't dress just right. So guess what their image of God is? To them, God is mad, He's really ugly and He's looking to judge you when you do something wrong. *Watch out, or God will thump you!* they think.

"God will thump you!" I actually heard that in a Bible study I once visited. "When you mess up, God will thump you!" this hard-boiled teacher said. So I asked, "What does God do when He thumps you?" See, my dad was a carpenter. He had big, ol' fingers like hammers. And every once in a while when we messed up, Dad would really let us have it. *Bam!* So I wondered what *thump* meant.

To this teacher, thumping meant everything that I have mentioned: car wrecks and other accidents, cancer, disease and judgment upon judgment. This sure wasn't any God I wanted to know! The image of the God I knew before I came to Christ acted like that. But that's the image so many Christians get in their minds *after* they come to Jesus. Why? Because it's the image their pastor grew up under. People with this image of God are likely to say,

"God took your parents."

"God gives you cancer."

"God doesn't want you to be pretty."

"God doesn't want you to have fun."

You get an ugly image of a God like this and you will become an ugly, judgmental person. People who live in that kind of religious environment are some of the most critical, judgmental, mean, prejudiced people on the face of the planet. I've heard some of them say, "Why, if you're not in our church, you're not even saved! If you're not in our denomination, you're not even a Christian. If you don't believe our way, you're wrong and are going to hell."

I remember reading what a popular preacher once printed in his newsletter. It was in regard to a very popular Christian music group, and he sent it all over America. It said, "I saw demons coming out of the speakers. Every rapper and rock musician who calls himself or herself a Christian just has a deceiving spirit of the devil."

This man had an image problem. He was a critical, judgmental, narrow-minded religious person.

When Jesus showed up on the earth, there were only two groups of people who really upset Him: the Pharisees and Sadducees. Their god was old, mean, nervous and full of hate. And they were just like him. They were legalistic and judgmental. They loved the praise of men more than the praise of God. They grappled for position and control.

The Pharisees and Sadducees hated and killed Jesus in part because His message was, "God is a loving God. He's not judging you. God just wants to be your Father. God sends no one to hell; people like you do that all by themselves. Your Father in heaven wants everyone, you included, to be in heaven with Him."

But the Pharisees had become like the image of their god. And when Jesus told them their image was wrong, they killed Him for it.

IMAGE IS AS IMAGE DOES

Your image of God will control how you conduct your life. Remember when God commanded Israel to possess the land? He said, "You can do it." But the Israelites said, "We're like grasshoppers in our own sight." Consequently, they were like grasshoppers in the enemy's sight and they died in the wilderness. (Num. 13:33.)

That was all tied to their image of God! They had seen the mighty miracles that delivered them out of Egyptian bondage. But while Moses, who had led them, was away receiving the Law for forty days, Exodus 32:1 tells us what the people did:

> **The people gathered together to Aaron, and said to him, "Come, make us gods that shall go before us; for as for this Moses, the man who brought us up out of the land of Egypt, we do not know what has become of him."**

Listen, a cow is good for two things—milk and beef. And a calf is worth even less than that. But when you read Israel's Old Testament history, you will find the idol of the calf replacing God in the northern kingdom.

If you go to India today, you will find calf worship and people starving to death while they worship beef. It happened back in Egypt too, but we don't see it in Scripture until Exodus 32.

Cattle as an idol may not be that popular in America today, but America's own brand of golden calves are all over the place. If we don't tell people who the true God is, they are going to worship something.

Today the spiritual seekers of the world have their own "angels." All this folklore and spooky stuff that's come out about angels wasn't around ten years ago. It's twisted; it's not biblical. You can also tune into the world's new religious broadcasts and pay them $4 a minute to talk with their psychic hot line. You didn't see many of these around ten years ago either. And it's because we haven't told people the truth!

But back to Moses. He was gone for forty days, and Israel chose to make their own golden calf. *So what if Moses had worked all those signs, wonders and miracles!* they seemed to think. After he had been gone for six weeks they were saying, "Let's make our own god. We don't know what happened to this guy."

So Aaron said, "Take off your golden earrings." That's right—Aaron, the one who stood by Moses every step of the way in confronting Pharaoh and working miracles said this! What he should have said was, "What in the world is wrong with you crazy people?" But instead he went right along with the crowd. Exodus 32:4-6 says:

> [Aaron] **received the gold from their hand, and he fashioned it with an engraving tool, and made a molded calf. Then they said, "This is your god, O Israel, that brought you out of the land of Egypt!"**
>
> **So when Aaron saw it, he built an altar before it. And Aaron made a proclamation and said, "Tomorrow is a feast to the Lord."**
>
> **Then they rose early on the next day, offered burnt offerings, and brought peace offerings; and the people sat down to eat and drink, and rose up to play.**

Can you imagine this? These people who saw the Red Sea divided made a calf to replace the God who delivered them! Not a bull! Not even a cow! Not a lion! Not a tiger! A *calf!* A good-for-nothing calf! You can't milk or breed a calf. It's nothing! It's a calf!

So here's the point. When men create their own gods, it's *always* good for nothing. According to Satan's mocking, evil intent, the false images of his deceptive worship will always minimize God's reality and limit man's abilities.

"This calf is our god!" the Israelites started saying. They traded the miraculous God of their supernatural deliverance for a worthless calf. It was as if they said, "Forget about those astounding miracles that destroyed the Egyptians and set us free—today our god is a puny, worthless cow!" Then they built an altar to worship and make offerings to it.

In the meantime, God revealed the idolatry to His man, Moses. He said, "Moses, get down there because your people have messed up again." (Ex. 32:7.)

Now, you know that when God says, "*Your* people, Moses, have messed up," He's ticked. It's like when Dad comes home and Mom says, "*Your* kids need some attention." When Moses "got home," he burned up the people's god, ground it to powder, put it in the water and made them drink it.

Can you imagine how one man could grind up those thousands of people's god and make them drink it? Well, Moses did. Then he called for those who would remain faithful to the Lord, and the faithful slaughtered the 3,000 others who chose to stay in their idolatry.

So the importance of seeing and honoring God for who He really is simply can't be overstated. When you make something your god, you become weak, small and limited. Then when you talk about your god— if you even do—others will get your image of who God is supposed to be. You end up trying to make a living and hang on until the Rapture— which you think will come tomorrow—to get out of this mess.

But when you serve *the* God of the Bible and have a true image of Him, you will be big, strong and powerful.

Okay, so much for the deceptive, negative images of God that men allow in their hearts. We've spent enough time on the devil's image counterfeits. So now let's take a look at the true image of God. And to do that I want to start with your own current view.

What's your image of God? Is your image of Jesus some young blond-haired, blue-eyed, spaced-out dude with a sheep under His arm? Or is He a mighty God, commanding a generation and bringing abundant life to them? Let's get a right image of God—no graven images. Let's see Him as He really is: loving, kind, gracious, big, abundant.

THE GOD OF ABRAHAM, ISAAC, JACOB AND *JOHN*

If there was ever anyone who walked intimately with God, it was the beloved apostle John. And in 1 John 3:8 he writes: **For this purpose the Son of God was manifested, that He might destroy the works of the devil.** In 1 John 4:8 he writes: **He who does not love does not know God, for God is love.**

John was with Jesus when He forgave the adulteress (John 8:1-12); healed and miraculously fed the masses (Matt. 4:23-25; 14:14-21); blessed the little children (Luke 18:16); and when Jesus laid His life down, John was there at the foot of the cross. (John 19:26.)

So John knew the God who'd called him to a life of ministry. His image of God was one of compassion, miraculous power and uncompromising love. And in 1 John 4:17 he writes, **As He is, so are we in this world.**

As *He* is, so are you in this world! You're not the product of evolution. Your hundred-thousand-year-old granddaddy was not some ape. You were made in the image of God. That image was modeled for us in the ministry of Jesus, and as He is, so are we *now*—not when we get to heaven, not after the Rapture. No—**As He is, so are we** [now] **in this world.**

But we will never be as *He is* until we truly know *who* and *how* He is now. Paul says we can know this through the renewing of our minds.

> **Put on the new man who is renewed in knowledge according to the image of Him who created him.**
>
> Colossians 3:10

This is important, because how you see Jesus and how He sees you will determine how you act.

MADE IN THE IMAGE OF THE LAST ADAM

Paul gives some spiritual insight into the Christian's true image through the resurrection truths in 1 Corinthians 15:45-49.

> And so it is written, "The first man Adam became a living being." The last Adam became a life-giving spirit. However, the spiritual is not first, but the natural, and afterward the spiritual. The first man was of the earth, made of dust; the second Man is the Lord from heaven. As was the man of dust, so also are those who are made of dust; and as is the heavenly Man, so also are those who are heavenly. And as we have borne the image of the man of dust, we shall also bear the image of the heavenly Man.

In this passage, Paul tells us that the first man, Adam, was natural, and that all natural men bear his image. Then he tells us that the "last Adam," Jesus, is the Lord of heaven, and that all who receive Him bear His image.

What Paul means is that as humans we are all like Adam in our natural bodies, but when we are born again, we become like Jesus in our spiritual beings; **and as is the heavenly Man, so also are those who are heavenly** (v. 48). So we should have *His* attitude, His perspective and His lifestyle, because we are made in His image.

Paul tells us in Romans 8:29:

> For whom He foreknew, He also predestined to be conformed to the image of His Son, that He might be the first-born among many brethren.

Now, that's powerful truth.

God made up His mind to send His last Adam in order to conform the Church to His Son's spiritual image. Now, that is heavy. The problem with so much of Christianity is not conforming; we want to put it off until heaven. We say, "Oh, yeah, I agree with everything the Bible says, so when I get to heaven, I'm gonna be just like Jesus." No! No! I say a thousand times no!

John didn't say, "As He is, so shall we be one day in heaven." No, John says, "As He is, so *are* we in this world!" Jesus taught His disciples to pray, **Thy kingdom come**—not, "Thy kingdom, I'm coming"! (Matt. 6:10 KJV).

So if the Church is going to ever walk in the image of our loving Creator, we will simply have to stop putting it off! There aren't a whole lot of sinners in heaven who need your witness. There aren't a whole lot of sick folks up there who need you to lay hands on them for their healing.

Now is the day of salvation. Now is the acceptable hour. There are millions of people who live around you right now who are sad, sick and sorrowful, and you're their only answer.

But instead of helping them, so many Christians are only trying to figure out how to pay their rent. Instead of reaching out and teaching the lost, they're trying to figure out how to get their kids out of bed on time.

So many of us get caught up mumbling and bumbling in the dirt of the world because that's how we see ourselves. Remember, **As [a man] thinks in his heart, so is he** (Prov. 23:7). What a person believes in his heart is what he expects. And what a person expects determines how he will live.

Why don't you have the money to go on a mission trip? We live in the richest country in the world, so what's the problem? "Well, I have bills," you say.

That's the image you've grown up with—barely getting by, just paying your bills. And when you get a little extra money, it's either gone quickly or you put it away for retirement at sixty-two. Jesus doesn't think like this. So we need to start thinking like Him.

The Church could do so much if we didn't spend all our energy *surviving!* We could help so many people if we didn't spend all our energy trying to help ourselves! In my church we constantly have to recruit prayer partners to pray with new converts, because two-thirds of the congregation doesn't have enough time to help a new convert! And we're not exclusive.

It is amazing to me that the majority of people in the body of Christ don't have enough time, knowledge, passion or power to help a new convert. The pastor can get them to the altar, but there are never enough church members to pray with them, because they have to be the first out of the sanctuary to get the roast out of the oven or a good table down at the cafeteria. They have to get home to their baseball games or to watch their movies. That's not thinking like Jesus would in this world.

So many of us live in our own little worlds because we've never been changed into the image of God. I'm not trying to put anyone down; I'm just trying to say that it's good when you can get up on God's mountain-top, where the air is thin and the view is good. It's good when you stop living down in the valley, where you're just trying to survive. And that's where the god of this world wants you, so he can get you to waste your life just trying to make ends meet.

BLINDED BY DARKNESS

Satan confuses the reality of God in the minds of Christians and non-Christians alike. He is the one who works overtime to blind us from the evidence in creation of God's existence. He was there to convince Israel that God had abandoned them at the foot of Horeb and that they should instead build a golden calf to worship. And he is here now to deceive any who will believe his lies.

Second Corinthians 4:3-4 says,

> **But even if our gospel is veiled, it is veiled to those who are perishing, whose minds the god of this age has blinded, who do**

not believe, lest the light of the gospel of the glory of Christ, who is the image of God, should shine on them.

Let me give you an example of one of Satan's lies. I think it takes more faith to believe that mankind and God's wonderful creation "happened" accidentally—as Satan's lie of evolution says—than it does to believe God spoke it into existence. There is more evidence for creation than there is for evolution. But it's all in the mind, or how we perceive God and His creation that surrounds us.

The devil is out there, stirring up his own brand of "faith" and blinding unbelievers' minds so that they believe God is nature or mother earth or a philosophy, a bird, a homosexual or a man Himself. Many refuse to believe in God, so they believe a theory like evolution because they are blind. And then the glory of God, which is the image of God, can't shine through those blind unbelievers.

GOD IS NOT OLD, MEAN AND NERVOUS

There are so many in the Church who have been blinded into thinking that God is mean and He is out to get anyone who steps over the line. The image of His glory can't shine through blinded religious thinking. That's why the Pharisees and Sadducees couldn't see Jesus' image shining forth. That's why so much of the Church today can't see it. Satan doesn't want people to see God's glorious image, so he keeps people blinded. And boy, do those blinded by Satan whip up some great excuses and rationalizations!

"Well, that's good that the pastor's all fired up," one of them might say. "But he doesn't understand me. He might be able to live that way, but he doesn't know what I've been through. I'm different. I'm special."

These are the thoughts and sayings of the devil, the god of this world, blinding the minds of unbelievers and keeping them from seeing the image of God and the glory of Christ which is all around them. But he also does it to Christians, who have the glory of Christ already resident within them!

Christ *in you*, the hope of glory is how Paul relates the glory of God that is inside a Christian (Col. 1:27). When you begin to see Him in you and yourself in Him, you will also begin to understand that you are like Him. Scripture declares that you are recreated in the likeness and image of God!

> **Therefore, if anyone is in Christ, he is a new creation; old things have passed away; behold, all things have become new. Now all things are of God, who has reconciled us to Himself through Jesus Christ, and has given us the ministry of reconciliation.**
>
> **2 Corinthians 5:17,18**

Of course, understanding these truths will begin to change the way you act.

When you discover the true image of God living in you, all of a sudden, that guy who cut you off on the freeway isn't worth shaking your fist at anymore. All of a sudden, the kid who's so frustrating isn't worth your pulling your hair out over anymore. The reason you keep letting those little things get to you is that you don't know who you are in Christ.

But once you discover who you are in Christ, you will walk through life as a son or daughter of God in regal wisdom and composure. You will no longer think of paying the bills the same way you once did. Instead, you will start thinking about how to invest in missions and touch the world.

People who fight over someone's pulling in front of them in their car, quibble with a waitress over 25 cents or go on strike just to get more money, for example, don't have a proper image of God. And too much of that goes on with God's people in the Church.

So again, we must do as Paul tells us in Colossians 3:10:

Put on the new man who is renewed in knowledge according to the image of Him who created him.

What are you seeing when you look in the mirror? If you're seeing anything less than the image of Jesus, you must get renewed in knowledge according to the image of Him so you can begin to live this life of Christ. As long as you see yourself as a grasshopper, you will be a grasshopper! (Num. 13:33.) If you're always saying, "Oh, I'm just trying to pay my bills; I'm just trying to make it through life; I'm just hanging on for the Rapture, you will waste your life. You will spend all of your time trying to figure out how to come up with a lease payment for your new car. You'll spend more time on your hair color than on missions. And you will continue to surround yourself with the golden-calf idols of the world as you spend more energy trying to get an approval on that mortgage than on caring for lost souls.

But there is a better way. God has promised us an abundant life, full of His promises and replete with His glory. Abundance, not lack. Glory, not darkness. And it all starts and ends with how you interpret His image. Remember, Romans 1:20 tells us God's **invisible attributes are clearly seen, being understood by the things that are made.**

If the attributes of God's character and divine nature can be seen in His creative genius that surrounds us naturally, how much more should that inspire us to seek Him in the truth of His Word! The Church has had enough blinding "sermonettes" that keep them little Christianettes, little babies who can go home and climb in their bassinets. It's time to get changed!

So in the chapters that follow we will study the process that every Christian man and woman is called to participate in. We will look at mind renewal and what I call the "great exchange" of giving our old man to God and putting on the new man.

As you stay faithful to read and work the action steps in each chapter, you will invite the glorious image of God's will and presence into your life.

3

Many born-again believers don't even realize how the bondage problems of their past keep them bound. So it's time for a new image. It's time to see ourselves becoming part of Christ's glorious Church! We need to see ourselves as God sees us and renew our self-image. And to start looking at this process, let's read what I call Paul's "glorious change" passage in 2 Corinthians 3:7-18:

> But if the ministry of death, written and engraved on stones, was glorious, so that the children of Israel could not look steadily at the face of Moses because of the glory of his countenance, which glory was passing away, how will the ministry of the Spirit not be more glorious?
>
> For if the ministry of condemnation had glory, the ministry of righteousness exceeds much more in glory. For even what was made glorious had no glory in this respect, because of the glory that excels. For if what is passing away was glorious, what remains is much more glorious. Therefore, since we have such hope, we use great boldness of speech—unlike Moses, who put a veil over his face so that the children of Israel could not look steadily at the end of what was passing away. But their minds were blinded. For until this day the same veil remains unlifted in the reading of the Old Testament, because the veil is taken away in Christ. But even to this day, when Moses is read, a veil lies on their heart. Nevertheless when one turns to the Lord, the veil is taken away.

> Now the Lord is the Spirit; and where the Spirit of the Lord
> is, there is liberty. But we all, with unveiled face, beholding as in
> a mirror the glory of the Lord, are being transformed into the
> same image from glory to glory, just as by the Spirit of the Lord.

Can you imagine what it must have been like for Moses when he came down out of the glorious presence of God into the idolatrous sin of Israel at the foot of the mountain? It must have been like walking out of heaven into hell. The god of this world had blinded the minds of the Israelites from the glory of God they had witnessed during their miraculous deliverance from Egypt. They exchanged the glory of the incorruptible God for the image of a worthless calf, and they rejoiced and offered worship to it.

Sometimes I think God must see so many of us in the Church like that—dancing around our idols of carnal selfishness because of our own misconceptions of who He really is.

As we have seen in Romans 1:20, there is no excuse for not knowing who God really is. But for those of us who have received His Spirit, there is even less of an excuse because of the special revelation in His Word. Today all men and women can receive the ministry of God's Spirit. Today, **when one turns to the Lord, the veil** [the curtain of the Law that blocks the Spirit's presence] **is taken away** and the Word of God becomes a living epistle written on our hearts (2 Cor. 3:16).

The Word of God tells us plainly who God is and what He wants us to do. And for the believer who understands God's image properly, the adventure of changing from glory to glory should happen every day. The Spirit is the changer who brings the change to pass, but we must want to be changed.

Let's look again at 2 Corinthians 3:18, in which Paul describes our process of change in terms of looking in a mirror:

But we all, with unveiled face, beholding as in a mirror the glory of the Lord, are being transformed into the same image from glory to glory, just as by the Spirit of the Lord.

Now let's look at this passage in *The Message Bible* to get an expanded description of this process of change.

Whenever, though, they turn to face God as Moses did, God removes the veil and there they are—face to face! They suddenly recognize that God is a living, personal presence, not a piece of chiseled stone. And when God is personally present, a living Spirit, that old, constricting legislation is recognized as obsolete. We're free of it! All of us! Nothing between us and God, our faces shining with the brightness of his face. *And so we are transfigured much like the Messiah, our lives gradually becoming brighter and more beautiful as God enters our lives and we become like him.*

I love this passage. The concept of my becoming brighter and more beautiful as I see God is thrilling to me. As He gets brighter and clearer in my mind and heart, He also becomes bigger—and a bigger part of my life. And as He becomes brighter in my life, I start looking and living more like Him.

The *King James Version* says we are changed from glory to glory, or from presence to presence. As we discussed, that's what *glory (doxa)* means: "presence."[1] God is bright and full of abundance. The glory of God is His presence in our world and in our lives. As we see Him clearly, we become like Him, His way of thinking and living becomes ours, His presence and goodness shines through us. This is how we are changed into His image; we take on a new self-image.

There is more to life than paying the bills, making the mortgage payments, gaining weight and getting closer to the grave! Our purpose, our destiny, is to be conformed to the image of Jesus. (Rom. 8:29.) God has offered us His presence, His glory, in a bright life of abundance.

That truth is what gets me up in the morning, makes me happy and gives me reason to breathe!

Every day you should want to become more and more like Him, being transformed from glory to glory and becoming brighter and more beautiful as God further enters your life. That's what it's all about. When that happens, you enjoy better relationships, make more money, have more influence and live on a higher level of life. Your life is more fulfilling, and you also fulfill your predestined purpose of being conformed to the image of Jesus.

A life of conforming to Christ's image is the life every Christian is called to live. So get your eyes off just trying to get to the next level in your company or getting that new car. Get your eyes on becoming more like Him, and you will find yourself at the next level in the company. You will find that you can have any car you want—or anything else— because God is working in you, making your life become brighter and more beautiful.

There Is More to Life Than Bills and Struggling

You see, life isn't supposed to be a daily struggle to pay the bills. And when we come to church, we shouldn't be looking for a "shot in the arm" to help us endure another week. It's not my intent as pastor of Christian Faith Center to be some kind of medic who dispenses a shot of spiritual medication to get the congregation through another week. No, we meet to rise a little higher in our lives, to grow a little larger in our hearts and to gain more wisdom and understanding for tomorrow.

My intent at every meeting is to exalt the goodness of God and explore the best that God has for us. I intend to honestly represent the glorious image of God and our opportunity to grow up into it. When we, God's people, have a proper image of who we are in the Lord, our attitudes should get better. Our sensing God's presence should get stronger. Our decisions should get sharper. Our marriages should get better, with more love and compassion every day. And our kids should grow wonderfully.

All of this should be happening because we're saying, "Yes, as I've been talking to God face to face every day at home, on the job and in church, I'm becoming brighter and more beautiful because the glory of God has not been blinded from my mind. He is freely entering my life, and I am becoming like Him."

When old friends see you, they should be saying, "You seem happier than I remember you. You seem more graceful than I remember. It seems like you have more dignity than I remember. What's happened to you?"

"Oh, I'm becoming brighter and more beautiful as I behold the image of God in my life. I'm becoming more like Him," you can answer.

If all your old friends can say when they see you is, "Well, you gained twenty pounds and lost your hair," that's bad, because that's not what life is all about. We're not supposed to be moping around, sagging, tired old Christians saying, "Oh, Lord Jesus, come quickly. Get me out of this mess!" No! We're supposed to be getting brighter and more beautiful, transformed from glory to glory into the image of God.

Why are so many Christians struggling with the day-to-day issues just as the world does, when they've been predestined to be conformed to the image of Jesus Christ? Why are so many Christian husbands and wives fighting, struggling with bills and their weight while their kids are running to the devil? Why are they going through the same problems the unsaved neighbors next door are going through?

Why?

Image. The god of this age has blinded their minds, and they can't see or believe the true glory and image of God. They are limited and held back. Even though they are on their way to heaven, hell is controlling their life.

So let's start looking at Satan's blinding process and how we get free of it to live from glory to glory. Let's look at 2 Corinthians 4:1-7:

> Therefore, since we have this ministry, as we have received mercy, we do not lose heart. But we have renounced the hidden things of shame, not walking in craftiness nor handling the word of God deceitfully, but by manifestation of the truth commending ourselves to every man's conscience in the sight of God.
>
> But even if our gospel is veiled, it is veiled to those who are perishing, whose minds the god of this age has blinded, who do not believe, lest the light of the gospel of the glory of Christ, who is the image of God, should shine on them.
>
> For we do not preach ourselves, but Christ Jesus the Lord, and ourselves your servants for Jesus' sake. For it is the God who commanded light to shine out of darkness who has shone in our hearts to give the light of the knowledge of the glory of God in the face of Jesus Christ.

But we have this treasure in earthen vessels, that the excellence of the power may be of God and not of us.

First of all, Paul tells us in verse 2 that if you want to walk in the high life of God's glory, you need to "renounce the hidden things of shame" and decide to live an upright life. The Holy Spirit is here to help us do that—always. Then, in verses 3 and 4, he reveals Satan's deceptive veiling of God's truth.

Paul isn't only talking in this verse about unbelievers who eternally perish. He is also talking about the false image some Christians have of God. If Christians' minds are blinded from the glorious image of God, they may be on their way to heaven, but they will be controlled by the god of this age until they get there.

For example, if you believe in Jesus as your Savior, but you don't believe in "that tithing stuff" because you don't think you can afford to, or you don't want any preacher to "get your money," then you just might go through life living from paycheck to paycheck.

If you don't believe in "that praying in other tongues stuff" because it seems just too weird or because you think it passed away long ago, then you may never understand the power of God while you're on earth.

If you don't think God wants to heal everybody, you may go through life sick and weak. You might even say, "Why, I know Sister Betsy, and she was a good Christian. She died!" Maybe you'd also say, "I'm not into casting out spirits and all. I don't even want to talk about all that stuff." Blind, blind, blind!

There is so much of the gospel that these kinds of Christians won't believe because their minds have been blinded to the glory of God's true image. When it comes to participating in the body as servants in the Church, blinded Christians will say, "Well, I don't have time for that."

When believers' minds get blinded to the point at which heaven is the only Christian reality they can see, the god of this age is then able to control their lives. Maybe they accept the New Testament mentally, but they don't participate in it. So from Monday to Saturday they function like the world. They struggle and deal with issues just like the world does. Then when Sunday rolls around, they nod their heads in approval at everything we pastors preach. But the glorious truth of the gospel isn't affecting their lives, so they aren't being changed from glory to glory.

It's not that our brothers and sisters who allow themselves to fall into this trap are bad people. It's not that they've been predestined to some negative position in life. It's not their IQ, their husband or wife, kids or something in their marriage; it's the god of this world. And it really angers me! Jesus died to make His followers new creations, and the god of this world blinds so many from the basics of Bible truth.

But now, what would happen to these same Christians if the light of the message of the glory of God, the image of Christ, were to shine on them? I'll tell you what would happen: They would be transformed into the image of Christ. Once born-again believers begin to see the good and loving image of our big, compassionate God, they will be transformed into that image from glory to glory. But too often this isn't the case.

There are so many false and worthless images of God in the Church today. Remember what the Israelites did at the foot of Mount Horeb? They broke one of the commandments which Moses had just received and made a worthless calf to worship.

Now, how can human beings do such foolish stuff? How can you hear the God of the universe talk to you personally, see the amazing plagues, watch the pillar of fire and the cloud, eat the miraculous manna and see the water miraculously flow out of the rock—and then turn right around and forget it ever happened? Aaron said, "Behold your god!" (Ex. 32:4.) And what was it? A golden calf.

As I said before, you'd think they could have come up with something better than a calf! Why not a majestic lion even?

So here again is the reality of making an idol. When you create a false image of God, it will always be less than what God truly wants for you in life. A false image of God will never get believers to the level of life that God wants them to have. Many don't come to Christ in the first place because they believe that if they were to live by God's "rules" in the Bible, they would have to give up so much. That's the god of this world blinding their minds. But it also happens to Christians after they're saved. Blinded Christians say, "If I really get committed, I'll lose my free time. I'll lose some money, or I might have to give up some other good stuff." They worship the same small image of that phony golden calf.

If your image of God is small, warped or perverted in some way, your mind is blinded to the things of God. Why do people starve in

India with cows walking all over the place? Because their image of God is so perverted that they actually think the cow is a reincarnated being. It could be their brother, so they won't eat it. It could even be god in their thinking; they don't know.

But Satan certainly knows, and he must snicker at people's deception from the cradle to the grave. When your mother tells you that early in life that the cow is holy and everything around you was once someone or something else, that part of your mind could stay blinded for the rest of your life.

You may think the idea of reincarnation sounds funny, but the same kind of "early blinding" happens in Christian homes. When a little boy or girl is told by parents and preachers that God is mean and angry, it is hard to shake that image. We still have a number of those now grown fire-and-brimstone types who preach a God who is ugly and mean: "*God's* gonna get you!" they say.

Listening to that, you'd think, "*Wow, God is really ticked off.*" Not only would you think that, but the world around us sees this image.

A while back my wife, Wendy, was telling a man on an airplane about my ministry. "My husband's in the ministry, and he teaches on television and so forth," she said. This fellow remarked, "Oh, is he one of those angry preachers?"

Now, listen, this man wasn't a Christian, but his understanding of the average preacher was ugly and ranting-and-raving mad. So it's bad enough that we in the Church hold on to such a negative image of God, but it gets even worse when we pass it along to unbelievers.

We serve the God of the universe, who describes Himself as love. But since the world sees Christians as right-wing radicals who are judgmental, mean and mad, that's how they also see God. And much of it is our own fault!

So I challenge you who are reading this to rethink the blind spots in your life. Be thinking about those thought patterns of yours which may not be biblical.

Our image of God makes an impact on how we see ourselves and how we live. So as you think about any false idols still littering your mind, allow God today to bring you new thoughts.

To help you get started, think about this: The universe continues to grow today at the speed of light. Scientists are discovering planets and stars beyond what they ever guessed existed. You see, God flung this universe into existence!

When God spoke the universe into existence, He said, "This is good; this is a cool playground, but I'm not done." So He picked out one planet in the universe and said, "I'm going make this one unique." Of everything we have discovered in our discoveries in space, earth is the only planet with life as we understand it. Isn't that awesome? There's not even another planet with a bush growing on it. That's amazing! Now we may find one someday, but we haven't yet. Furthermore, scientists can't find another planet in the universe that has an atmosphere like ours. And believe me, they've been looking.

God created mankind and the earth we inhabit to be unique among the billions of other planets He flung into space. He created light, earth, water. Then He spent a few days with the lions, monkeys and fish. He swam with the dolphins and raced a few whales.

But the Lord said, "This isn't it yet. This isn't what I really want. I love the environment, but I need something more. So this is what I'll do: First, I will create a being who is like Me. (Gen. 1:26-28.) So he has to have a will. He must have a creative mind and be sovereign over his own life, because it is he who will determine where he will exist eternally."

So God created a being who could relate intimately to Him.

**"Let Us make man in Our image, according to Our
likeness...." So God created man in His own image; in the image
of God He created him; male and female He created them.**

Wow, that's pretty strong stuff. Mankind was made in the likeness
and image of God, so we're like God. Then He put man in Eden and
said, "Your job is to take care of the Garden and make it what you want
it to be. Have dominion, take control, build it, shape it, make it
whatever you want. Listen, guard it and keep it—it's up to you."

Then God just hung out! We don't know if it was every day or once a
week. But He was there with Adam and Eve as they went about their work.

We also know Adam was commissioned to name the animals and
that Adam was using 100 percent of his brain; he wasn't thinking all day
about what to call the mosquito. He was a sharp creation, who reigned
over all the earth.

I don't know, but maybe some of their conversations went like this:

"How's it going, Adam?"

"Oh, hello, God. Well, I've just been over here working on a theory
of nuclear fusion. I was trying to understand how You made this whole
universe work."

"Yes, well, since you asked, nuclear fusion takes place when this
happens and that happens. But that isn't as exciting as creating light. Let
me tell you about that..."

Whether any of their conversations went like this or not, I don't know.
But the point I want to make is that Adam, who was created in the
likeness and image of God, was very close to his Creator. They spent time
together, probably talking about everything from the most awesome scien-
tific theories to the intimacies of procreation between husband and wife.

But Adam chose to break that closeness when he betrayed their
relationship. (Gen. 3.) The act of eating from the Tree of the Knowledge

of Good and Evil was a matter of trust. God told Adam to restrict himself from that one tree only in the Garden and left him with a choice: obey or disobey. Obviously, it was good to obey and evil to disobey.

It's the same situation in any parent/child relationship. We don't care so much when our kids get in the cookie jar. But we do care when they disobey our command not to, breaking the honest trust in our relationship. We don't care necessarily that they stay out late running around the park, but we do if it's after we tell them to be home. We care about their trusting, believing and obeying us. And when they don't, the relationship suffers.

The issue is relationship. Christians get all hung up on what sins they commit, and they allow Satan to blind them into the image of their sin. Then they hide in guilt and fear from their relationship with God. God wants to be close to His people! What hurts Him is when our choices break down our fellowship with Him. When you hide, you have to "fake it" through life instead of just being open, honest and free.

So I challenge you to think about this—God created you for two reasons:

1. To be like Him.

2. To be close to Him.

That's all.

The serpent came to blind mankind's mind from the glory of this simple truth. He told Eve, "Why, if you would do this, you could be like God," *but Eve was already just like God!* So Satan gave her a new doctrine that deceived her into betraying her relationship with God. He perverted Eve's image and separated her from relationship.

This is why the enemy comes to blind born-again Christians' minds—to separate them from communion and intimate fellowship with God. Once he does that, he can corrupt the true goodness of God's image. I've talked with people Satan has done this to. They have many excuses—soccer games, hard days and weeks at work—you name it. So they stay home and watch the NFL on Sunday mornings. On Wednesday evenings, they mow the lawn. When you ask them where they've been during church they say, "Oh, I've just got so many things going on."

So the one thing God wants most out of man—relationship—gets perverted through Satan's blinding. We don't know we're like God because we don't have a clear picture of Him. And we don't want to be close to Him, because we get caught up in all our golden idols of legalism and self-serving mediocrity.

When you mention the powerful statement from 1 John 4:17 to most Christians—**As He is, so are we in this world**—most of them will simply blow it off.

Why? That kind of statement just doesn't fit the image Satan has passed on to them. In fact, if you go around saying, "As God is, so are we in this world," today's modern Pharisee will call you a New Age sorcerer. His image of God is angry and confused.

When you say the Church can do Christ's miraculous works, these bound-up religious puppets, who wait to pounce on anyone who doesn't believe just like they do, will brand you a heretic. But *Jesus* said it, not brother what's-his-name! He said, **"Most assuredly, I say to you, he who believes in Me, the works that I do he will do also; and greater works than these he will do, because I go to My Father"** (John 14:12). And Jesus is still saying that today.

Today the Lord is *still* saying, "If you walk with Me, if you believe in Me, you're going to be like Me." And this is *still* God's goal—for us to be like Him!

So we must get the religious traditions out of our minds! We must get all that nonsense about "holy poverty," punishment and all of that other unbiblical nonsense out of our Protestant heads. We must get a new image of God, who created us to be like Him. And I tell you, if you'll believe in Him, you will do everything He does!

What was Jesus like? Jesus was tough on religion and tender with folks. He walked victoriously in every circumstance. When people gathered around to accuse Him, He would make a statement that caused them to walk away, completely astounded.

When too many showed up for lunch, He multiplied a boy's lunch to feed thousands—with twelve baskets left to spare. When His disciples couldn't catch any fish, He said, "Cast the net over there," and they pulled in a net-breaking, boat-sinking load.

When a little woman with an issue of blood came and touched the hem of His garment He said, "Woman, your faith has made you well."

Everywhere Jesus went, He healed and fed folks and answered their problems. Everything He did was victorious. Remember, it was Jesus who said, **He who believes in Me, the works that I do he will do also; and greater works than these he will do, because I go to My Father** (John 14:12).

Now, when you go preaching this verse around a group of Christians who have a right image of God, they will say, "I know that's a tall order, Pastor Treat, but if Jesus said it, I believe it. So I will lay hands on the sick when they cross my path. I will give myself to His Word and calling as His Spirit convicts me to do His works."

Walking out the reality of our Christian life is learning how to be brighter and more beautiful, going from glory to glory! God hasn't left us alone in this life with only steeples and man-made religion. He gave us Jesus as our Savior, deliverer and role model. Our Father in heaven wouldn't have done that if He intended us to fail. He wants us to learn daily how to live this life of Christianity like Jesus lived it. And He gave us Himself to make it come true.

When you study Jesus' words further along in John, you see what I mean: **At that day you will know that I am in My Father, and you in Me, and I in you** (John 14:20). When Jesus sent the Holy Spirit, He came into our lives. And we are living in the day in which we can know that He is in the Father and in us and that we are in Him.

I'm telling you, all God wants to do is hang out with and be close to us like He was with Adam! He wants to live in the midst of us so He can teach us how to reign in Jesus' name.

When you see Jesus as He really is, you begin to see who you can really be. And all of a sudden, life is no longer about paying bills or getting ticked off at the neighbor's barking dog. When you see God as He really is, you no longer put value on the priorities of the world. You begin to think differently because the god of this world can't blind your mind.

When we see Jesus as He really is, our former golden-calf idols of the world marketers stop controlling us. The sports teams don't control our schedule. The news doesn't control our emotions. The economy doesn't control our finances. All that happens because the golden calf that blinded us has been ground up. When we realize that the Father is in Jesus, Jesus is in us and we're in Him, it changes everything.

When we step into the office, people say, "That guy's different." When they see your children, they say, "How do you parent them so well?" When they see our prospering, they say, "How'd you close that deal? I worked on it for a year and couldn't get it!" But you step in with a new image, a new spirit, that's brighter and more beautiful. He's in you. You're in Him. The world says, "Wow!"

So let's move along now into the transformational process that renews our minds and gets us thinking like this. The veil of legalism and tradition has been removed. Now it's time for a new image. It's time to move forward and be like Jesus. It's time to become Christ's glorious Church!

4

SPIRIT AND SOUL SALVATION: THE CHRISTIAN'S KINGDOM KEYS

I'm about to share some important keys with you that, if you will invest the time and energy necessary to absorb, I believe will enable you to discover your God-ordained destiny and the biblical truths you need to change and grow. I have developed steps designed to thoroughly acquaint you with spiritual mind renewal. I challenge you to spend enough time to fully consider, reflect and in some cases memorize this important material.

Whatever your present place in life, you have the potential to move forward and experience more of God's will and plan. You may be starting with an element of success in life, or you may be starting at the foundational level. Wherever you are, let's move forward together toward God's best and your destiny.

RENEWING THE MIND KEY NUMBER 1:

YOU CAN CHANGE TO MAKE YOUR LIFE WHAT YOU WANT IT TO BE

Renewing the mind is a journey I've been on for the past twenty-five years, so I know how important it is to think and pray through the programming of the "computer" that we call the human mind. I've gone from being an average American teenager who didn't like himself or anything about life to being a husband, father and pastor who enjoys the blessing of the Lord in every way.

The truths you will learn in the following pages are neither my ideas or thoughts, nor are they the hype of another self-help message; they are principles from the Word of God.

I learned long ago that if you have a map of the wrong city, then no matter how good your attitude, how positive your confession or how positive your spirit, you will stay lost, never arriving at your desired destination.

There are dozens of uplifting and positive teachers and writers among us today, but most don't give you the right principles to be truly positive. Once you have the right map, you can use your positive attitude, positive confession and positive spirit to effectively move you toward the goals of your life. The Bible provides us with such direction.

The Bible is God's map of principles that will get us where we want to go—both in day-to-day living and eternally. All the philosophies of the world have proven inadequate and bring failure. The world's broken marriages, children, economy and nations are evidence of that. And while the Word of God may not be popular, it *alone* gives the principles that guide human beings on how to have happy families, healthy lives and fulfilled destinies. If we will renew our way of thinking according to the principles in the Bible, we will find the success in life we so desperately need.

I believe every Christian and even most non-Christians desire to change their lives and find a higher way; but they often doesn't know how and feel unable to.

The fact is, you *can* change and be all God planned for you to be. He has predestined you for greatness spiritually, mentally, physically and financially. Your marriage, family, career and self-esteem can be exciting and fulfilling.

Are you ready to start your journey? Good. Then let's get started by reviewing the basics of spiritual conversion by examining what it truly means to be born again.

Spirit Versus Soul Salvation: There Is a Difference

As we have already discussed in great detail, there is more to God's plan of salvation than going to church, saying a prayer (which I did many times in jail) or becoming religious. One of the first lessons I learned as I began to build a new life in the mid-seventies was that my spirit was separated from God's Spirit.

You would think this basic truth was common knowledge, but many church buildings today are filled with people who don't understand this simple, basic spiritual knowledge. To really change my life, I learned of my need for a relationship with the One who created and destined me to fulfill my calling in life. And I discovered that I couldn't have a relationship with God until I was reborn from above.

So my first step was to be spiritually saved, or born again. To be born again is to be spiritually recreated. It has nothing to do with the way today's religionists, New-Age gurus and motivational speakers are teaching it. And it must be distinguished from soul salvation, which we will look at later.

You Must Be Born Again

In John 3:3,6 Jesus said, **"Most assuredly, I say to you, unless one is born again, he cannot see the kingdom of God.... That which is born of the flesh is flesh, and that which is born of the Spirit is spirit."**

Paul expanded on Jesus' teaching in 2 Corinthians 5:17: **Therefore, if anyone is in Christ, he is a new creation; old things have passed away; behold, all things have become new.**

Suddenly, at the age of nineteen, I realized that there was so much more to life than mere physical birth. I was blessed with the knowledge of God's promised new birth. And since the new birth is man's entryway into God's abundant life, I want to review it as our first renewal step.

You are a spirit being who lives in a physical body. Your body is alive, but until the "second" or new birth—until you've been born again—your spirit man on the inside is dead, or *separated,* from God. It exists, but it can't contact the Father and you have no relationship with Him. You may believe in God, attend church, know about God and have religious behavior; but Jesus said you must be born again or you will never see, experience and be part of the kingdom of God. The new birth is God's kingdom key. In fact, James 2:19 tells us that even Satan's evil kingdom "believes" in the kingdom of God, but because they have no part in it, they can only tremble at God's power: **You believe that there is one God. You do well. The demons also believe—and tremble!**

When we are born again, our spirit is changed, and we become joined to the Holy Spirit. Second Corinthians 3:17 tells us, **Now the Lord is the Spirit; and where the Spirit of the Lord is, there is liberty.** In Romans 10:9-10 Paul says:

> **If you confess with your mouth the Lord Jesus and believe in your heart that God has raised Him from the dead, you will be saved [this is the new birth]. For with the heart one believes to righteousness, and with the mouth confession is made to salvation.**

This new beginning is a spiritual change, not a physical, or mental change. When you become a new creation, it is obvious that your body doesn't change. I still had red hair, was still 6 feet 3 inches and needed to exercise more. So if you are bald, overweight, skinny, muscular or weak before you are born again, you will still be bald, overweight, skinny, muscular or whatever after you're born again.

The same is true for the mind. I had the same fears, bad attitudes, questions, desires and thoughts after I was born again as I'd had before. Why? I did because this is not a physical or a mental process; it is a spiritual one. It is only your inner man—your spirit—that is changed in the new birth. The rest is up to your willingness to let God change you.

RENEWING THE MIND KEY NUMBER 2:

THE NEW BIRTH CHANGES YOUR SPIRIT—
RENEWING THE MIND CHANGES THE SOUL

Being born again is the beginning of God's plan of redemptive life, but sad to say, for most Christians, it's also the end when it comes to growing with God. Too many never learn the next step—which actually takes the rest of our lives here on earth to accomplish—and go on to Christian growth and spiritual maturity.

While your spirit is recreated *instantly* when you make Jesus the Lord of your life, your mind, which is part of the soul, must be changed through an *ongoing* process. It is not an instantaneous change. It takes commitment, determination and desire to bring it to pass. Making that change is called *renewing the mind.* And though it is the key to all Christian growth, most Christians do little of it because of a lack of knowledge or a lack of discipline.

Let me share a natural, physical example of this spiritual truth. I delivered our three children at home. Though my part was much easier than my wife, Wendy's (especially since Caleb was 10 pounds 10 ounces, Tasha was 10 pounds and Micah was six weeks early at 7 pounds), I can still testify that helping my wife birth those little critters was much easier than raising them. The birth took a matter of moments—but raising them has been an ongoing process of teaching, training and loving for many years.

So it is in the Christian life. To be born again and make a commitment to the Lord takes a matter of moments. But to move on from there to spiritual maturity requires a disciplined, daily growth process of teaching and training oneself. This process involves reprogramming your thoughts with the thoughts of God and exchanging the way you think in the natural to the way God says in His Word we should think.

In 1 Thessalonians 5:23, Paul says the Christian walk includes changes to the spirit, soul and body: **Now may the God of peace Himself sanctify you completely; and may your whole spirit, soul, and body be preserved blameless at the coming of our Lord Jesus Christ.**

Now the soul is your mind, emotions and will. If we are to walk with God and fulfill our destinies as Christians, we must deal with the whole person—spirit, body and soul.

Paul says we are to be sanctified "completely," or wholly. We must go beyond the new birth; getting saved is only the first step in spiritual development. Of course, we can't add to the complete work of salvation in a spiritual sense, but we can change our souls and, to some degree, our bodies. Put another way, salvation of the spirit man is an eternal work that can't be earned, improved or added to. But the *salvation of the soul* is another subject.

Ephesians 2:8-9 says, **For by grace you have been saved through faith, and that not of yourselves; it is the gift of God, not of works, lest anyone should boast.**

In this verse Paul tells us that no one can work for spiritual salvation; Jesus provided it as a gift. Those religions that have their people selling magazines, doing missions work or trying to earn some eternal blessing through prayers, candles, money or anything else just don't understand the work that Jesus did for all mankind. There is nothing anyone can do to deserve or improve upon the new birth. No one can be saved spiritually through works.

However, everyone who has been born again can and must work for the salvation of his soul. This was not a finished work at the Cross of Calvary. In fact, Paul says in 1 Corinthians 1:18, **For the message of the cross is foolishness to those who are perishing, but to us who are being saved it is the power of God.** And in Philippians 2:12 he writes, **Work out your own salvation with fear and trembling.**

In both of these verses Paul says we are saved through the message of the Cross and we are to work out our salvation beyond that. That is the growth and renewal process which enables us to experience all that God has for us.

James 1:21 says, **Therefore lay aside all filthiness and overflow of wickedness, and receive with meekness the implanted word, which is able to *save your souls*.**

Now, James is writing to spiritually saved Christians who also need to work out the soulish aspect of their salvation by receiving the Word of God in their lives. The Word of God reprograms the Christian's thinking by showing him how God thinks. And when Christians start thinking like God, their behavior lines up with their thinking.

Get a hold of this kingdom key, and it is sure to transform your life!

To help you record and work through the crucial process of spiritual mind renewal, I have provided Steps to Personal Transformation following many of the chapters. After each chapter studied, please plan to answer the questions and review the chapter material as a time of reflection.

Steps to Personal Transformation

1. When did I make Jesus the Lord of my life and experience the new birth? [If you are not born again, pray this prayer: "Heavenly Father, I confess Jesus as Lord of my life. I believe Jesus was raised from the dead. I turn away from the sin and negativity of my life and turn to Jesus to lead and guide my life. Thank You, Lord Jesus, for coming into my heart and giving me a new spirit. I will learn from You and follow You from this day forward."]

   _____

   _____

2. How have I renewed my mind since I was born again?

   _____

3. What three areas of my life most need renewal at this time?

   _____

   _____

4. Do I really want growth and change in my life?

   _____

5

The most powerful verse of Scripture God used in my first years as a Christian—and still uses—is Romans 12:2: **And do not be conformed to this world, but be transformed by the renewing of your mind, that you may prove what is that good and acceptable and perfect will of God.**

Through this verse, I learned that even though I'd become a Christian, I remained conformed to the world and all of its failure and problems until I renewed my mind.

RENEWING THE MIND KEY NUMBER 3:

YOU CAN BE ON YOUR WAY TO HEAVEN BUT LIVE IN HELL ON EARTH

Now, I was on my way to heaven because I had been born again, but I was learning that if I didn't start renewing my mind, I could live like hell until I got there.

So many Christians struggle through life with negative attitudes, sin, failures, divorce and depression and wonder why it's all happening to them. Some have built doctrines to explain their lifestyle of defeat. Their image of God and of themselves is very negative, so they blame their failures on the "sovereignty of God" in order to explain their troubles.

The fact is, they are still conformed to the world, and because their mind hasn't been renewed, they can't prove what is the good, acceptable and perfect will of God in their lives. The Lord says of this:

Let no one say when he is tempted, "I am tempted by God"; for God cannot be tempted by evil, nor does He Himself tempt anyone. But each one is tempted when he is drawn away by his own desires and enticed. Then, when desire has conceived, it gives birth to sin; and sin, when it is full-grown, brings forth death.

James 1:13-15

When our minds are renewed by the Word of God, we will overcome negative desires and live in God's perfect will.

If after they're born again, many Christians are still depressed and afraid of life's circumstances, if they're still treating their spouse badly, struggling in poverty, having sex with someone they aren't married to, caught up in pornography or generally mad at the world, then though they may be born again, they are still conformed to the world.

Some believe that if Christians were to ever sin in these ways, they couldn't be born again. But John says in his first epistle that we *will* sin but that we can *receive forgiveness* if we confess our sin to Jesus. (1 John 1:9.) Furthermore, if we say we never sin, we are *lying.* (v. 10.)

The point is that Christians will mess up but we can be forgiven. Through renewing the mind, we overcome those failures, and we don't have to live in them. We don't have to be conformed, fashioned, molded or controlled by the ways of the world. We can walk with God and be an example of His will.

The word *transformed* Paul uses in Romans 12:2 means to go through a complete change in form or kind. The Greek word used in this verse is *metamorphoo.*[2] It means to go through a complete change in form, such as the caterpillar does when it comes out of its cocoon, transformed into a butterfly. A caterpillar doesn't just add some wings to its furry, long body. It completely changes into a different kind of being that can do totally different things and live a totally different life.

The Christian who undergoes the Holy Spirit's metamorphosis will begin to see the fullness of his salvation. He will live a completely different life than before and accomplish great things when he is transformed by the renewing of the mind.

RENEWING THE MIND KEY NUMBER 4:

RENEWING THE MIND IS MORE THAN LEARNING; IT IS CHANGING

So many people come to church to learn something new. They want new intellectual insight and feel good if the sermon is stimulating, intriguing or exciting. But they never consider changing the way they think or live as a result of what they hear. They are so far away from changing that they really don't make a decision *not* to change; they just don't consider the subject and therefore never think about it.

For many, the Bible and church can be religious traditions that aren't a part of the real world and their daily lifestyles. So there must be some major adjustments in their thinking to get started in the renewing the mind process. Many Christians have been taught that if they just read their Bibles, pray and go to church regularly, they will become stronger Christians. But it's too bad we never examined the fruit of that thinking. The fact is, a multitude of people have done those things all their lives and aren't living happy, prosperous, successful Christian lives.

Romans 12:2 clearly shows us there is more to Christian living than what many think. It is possible to read the Bible, pray and go to church and yet never renew your mind. The person who sins all week but is a faithful church attender proves that. The pastor who preaches great sermons but is eventually caught in adultery proves that. Renewing the mind is so much more than going through religious motions. It is a conscious effort and labor to:

1. Become aware of how we really think and believe

2. Become aware of how God wants us to think

3. Focus our thoughts on God's thoughts

4. Practice the thoughts of God until they are our own

5. And live the thoughts of God in everyday life

This process must be repeated time and time again as we come into situations in which attitudes and thoughts arise that are contrary to the Word of God. It isn't an overnight change. Our transformation through the renewing of our minds can't be received by the laying on of hands. It is a lifestyle that we are invited to participate in.

RENEWING THE MIND KEY NUMBER 5:

RENEWING THE MIND IS A LIFESTYLE, NOT AN EXPERIENCE

If we ever want to see the good, acceptable and perfect will of God in our lives, we must get on with the renewing of our minds. Paul says this is the only way the necessary transformation can take place. Many Christians aren't seeing all of God's promises being fulfilled in their lives. Many who say they are Christians have no lifestyle to back it up. These things can only be changed through the transformation of their lives, and that happens by the renewing of the mind.

Most of us have areas in our lives that are going along pretty well. We have developed right thinking in those areas, and it seems as though we don't have as much trouble in them as in some other aspects of life. Some people do well with money but struggle with relationships. Others do well with family but struggle with their health. Then there are others who seem to be doing well in every aspect of life but carry secrets of fornication, pornography and the like.

We must be renewing our minds in every area of Christian life and realize that our being successful in one aspect doesn't necessarily mean we are successful. If I'm a great minister but lose my children to the world,

I'm not successful. I may be strong and have a renewed mind in certain areas, but I must press on to deal with every part of my thought life.

Second Corinthians 10:4-5 says:

> **For the weapons of our warfare are not carnal but mighty through God for pulling down strongholds, casting down arguments and every high thing that exalts itself against the knowledge of God,** *bringing every thought into captivity to the obedience of Christ.*

Strongholds are thoughts and attitudes that have such a grip on your mind that even though you don't want to think the way you do, you can't help it. You feel like your mind is controlling you, and you can't stop thinking certain ways.

There are many people who feel terrible about the things that go on in their minds and the things those thoughts cause them to do. We've all seen or heard of people who don't want to do the things they do but feel like they can't stop. The truth is, you can stop that thought process, but it must be done according to God's Word.

Paul says these kinds of thoughts must be overcome by bringing them captive to the obedience of the Word of God.

When a person is consumed by negative or worldly thinking, that can become a stronghold over a period of time.

The man who thinks about violence, cursing and "proving his manliness" will soon have a bad temper. He may even end up fighting with anyone who opposes him or steps on his pride.

The one who watches or reads pornography regularly will soon be consumed with sexual fantasies and desires that will control his thought life. He will be driven by lust to seek out ungodly and unnatural fulfillment, though he can never be fulfilled; he is trapped in a way of thinking that will destroy him.

The woman who watches soap operas may soon become unsatisfied with her husband and her life. Before long she might begin to fantasize about other men and living out the situations on the programs that fill her mind.

When a marriage of ten, twenty or thirty years ends in divorce, there may have been years of thoughts about other people that finally led to the divorce. Many of these thoughts come from the examples and messages that are put out by ungodly television shows and other media.

Jesus said we must be careful of what we hear, because we may soon be controlled by it, whether good or bad. Mark 4:24 says, **Take heed what you hear. With the same measure you use, it will be measured to you; and to you who hear, more will be given.**

This is why we must guard our minds and not allow negative strongholds to take control over us.

If negative strongholds had already been established before we became born again, we must go to work, capture every thought, and drive them out with the thoughts of God. Strongholds of fear, anger, poverty, low self-esteem, pride and selfishness continue to control many Christians years after they are saved. Though they have prayed about them and tried to get deliverance, the problem persists. And these things will never change in their lives until they are transformed by the renewing of their minds.

This is not to say that some bondage and negative behaviors in Christians aren't caused by demonic oppression. When there is a demonic stronghold the demon must be cast out. But even in these cases involving demonic activity, if there isn't a renewal of the mind, the enemy will come back. And Jesus said the end of that person will be worse than the beginning. (Matt. 12:43-45.)

Renewing the mind is an exciting journey of change and discovery that enables us to see God's will come to pass in our lives. There is no greater joy or fulfillment than to know we are fulfilling the perfect will of God. And there is no other way, according to the Bible, to prove the will of God in our lives than by the renewing of the mind. That is how we see God as He really is and how we grow up into His image.

STEPS TO PERSONAL TRANSFORMATION

1. What does the Bible mean when it says, **Be not conformed to this world?** _____

   _____

   _____

2. In what areas of my life am I still conformed to this world?

   _____

   _____

3. What is biblical transformation?

   _____

   _____

4. In what way is renewing the mind different than learning?

   _____

   _____

5. What things have I learned from the Lord but have not yet renewed or changed?

   _____

   _____

6

CHANGE IS A WAY OF LIFE

Reproofs of instruction are the way of life.

Proverbs 6:23

Reproofs, instruction, confrontation and corrections from the Word of God are designed to bring change to our lives. In Proverbs 6:23, Solomon tells us that change is a way of life. If we want to walk with God, know His perfect will and experience the fullness of His plan for our lives, we must change continually. This is the transformation that Paul is talking about in Romans 12:2. A lifestyle involving regular instruction and correction moves us forward in Christian growth.

Throughout the book of Proverbs, the words *reproof, reprove, rebuke, correct, instruct* and *teach* show us that to have the wisdom and ways of God, we must be willing to change. As I said earlier, renewing the mind is more than learning and changing oneself. It involves more than just gaining new insight or information. The process of change has as much to do with "taking off" as it does with "putting on." It involves both subtracting and adding.

In Ephesians 4:22-24 we read:

> **Put off, concerning your former conduct, the old man which grows corrupt according to the deceitful lusts, and be renewed in the spirit of your mind, and that you put on the new man which was created according to God, in true righteousness and holiness.**

RENEWING THE MIND KEY NUMBER 6:

RENEWING THE MIND INVOLVES TAKING OFF THE OLD CARNAL THOUGHTS OF THE FLESH, AND PUTTING ON THE NEW SPIRITUAL THOUGHTS OF GOD

God uses the principle of taking something off before He can put something on throughout the New Testament. Therefore, in the process of renewing the mind, we must realize that God does the same with us. There are as many thoughts and attitudes that need to be taken off as there are that must be put on. The process involves both give and take. It is possible to learn many good things, but it's just as possible to never take off the things that keep you from success.

The college graduate has more than enough knowledge to succeed in his area of study, but if he has a negative mind-set, he may not experience success.

The one who knows all about nutrition and exercise will still be overweight and out of shape unless he removes the negative thoughts and habits that created his unhealthy lifestyle.

It is obvious that just hearing or learning the truth is not all there is to being free. Jesus said that it is as we abide, or live, and continue in His Word that we will know the truth and that when we do this, the truth will set us free.

> **Then Jesus said to those Jews who believed Him, "If you abide in My word, you are My disciples indeed. "And you shall know the truth, and the truth shall make you free."**
>
> John 8:31-32

The word *know* in this verse means to understand in an experiential way.[1] Its use implies that something has been removed, taken out or taken off and then replaced by the truth. This is when the truth will really set you free.

So many Christians can quote Scriptures about finances, health, marriage or family, but they aren't free in these areas. Just learning a verse or a passage of Scripture doesn't mean you will be free. Old thoughts that aren't in line with the thoughts of God must be replaced or rejected by truth. The new man can't be put on without taking the old man off.

RENEWING THE MIND KEY NUMBER 7:

TAKING OFF THE OLD MAN IS AS
IMPORTANT AS PUTTING ON THE NEW

Let me give you an example of what I'm talking about. I've had the joy of being a father for the past fourteen years. At the writing of this edition, Caleb, our firstborn, is fourteen, Tasha is twelve and Micah is nine. As I mentioned earlier, Wendy and I delivered all three in our home (she did all the hard work; I just did the catching). It didn't take me long to learn that these little critters need plenty of attention, *especially* on one end of the anatomy! They were calling for a diaper change either by their smell or whines every couple of hours.

So every couple of hours, they would get a diaper change. Now, if I had sprinkled a little powder on that old diaper and put on a new one over it, their need wouldn't have been met. They weren't changed until the old diaper was taken off and the new one was put on. It wouldn't have taken long for the aroma of the dirty diaper to rise through the cover of the clean one if I had just covered the old one up.

Similarly, there are many Christians who want to put on the clean "diaper" of Christianity but don't want to deal with the dirty one that was there before the new birth. They put new thoughts in, but it's not long before the old thoughts start stinking up the new. And soon their lives are back in the same old problems.

They're like a park built on a garbage dump. The grass is pretty, and the flowers smell good; but it isn't long before the garbage begins to come through. You can't build a successful Christian life on the garbage dump of negative thinking. Change involves removing the old, as well as installing the new.

Remember the old saying, "Don't curse the darkness; light a candle"? This holds true when it comes to renewing the mind. Taking off the old and putting on the new are simultaneous changes. We can't sit down and try to make negative thoughts leave our mind. The whole time we are trying to make them leave, we're thinking on the thoughts we don't want. We must not spend our time trying not to think about the old thoughts of fear, anger, sin. Instead, we must learn to think on the things the Scripture commands. As we set our minds on God's thoughts, His truth will drive out the old.

In Philippians 4:8 Paul writes:

> **Finally, brethren, whatever things are true, whatever things are noble, whatever things are just, whatever things are pure, whatever things are lovely, whatever things are of good report, if there is any virtue and if there is anything praiseworthy— meditate on these things.**

The Amplified Bible says, **Fix your minds on them.** So, yes, we need to be aware of and resist our old carnal thoughts. But at the same time, we must give ourselves to meditating, pondering, focusing and fixing our minds on the thoughts of God.

Change isn't an easy thing. We are programmed from our childhood to believe that once we're out of school, we stop growing. Except for functional learning, we usually don't make any changes in our lifestyle. In fact, we build facades and images to act like we know everything, and we try not to change. We want to give the impression that we've got it all together and don't need to change.

Then there are the family traditions, religious traditions and just fleshly stubbornness that keep us from growing and changing. All these tendencies must be dealt with to make change a positive thing, not something we avoid.

RENEWING THE MIND KEY NUMBER 8:

CHANGE MUST BE A POSITIVE PART OF
OUR LIVES, NOT SOMETHING WE AVOID

The people of Israel didn't enter their Promised Land when they could have because they refused to change. The generation that came out of Egypt had a slavery mind-set and wouldn't change it. They murmured at the leadership of Moses and argued with the commands of the Lord. Though they had seen many miracles and had God's heavenly pillar of cloud and fire to guide them, they wouldn't let go of their old mentality.

As the Israelites stood on the border of the land that flowed with milk and honey, they listened to the evil report of the ten spies who had gone into the land. The land was theirs for the taking, but the multitude began to cry and murmur about the giants in the land. Joshua and Caleb, two spies with a good report, tried to lead them in faith to obey God, but the people refused.

We were like grasshoppers in our own sight, and so we were in their sight (Num. 13:33). They hadn't changed their way of thinking from their slave mentality in Egypt. Though God was with them, called them His people and promised to take them into the Promised Land, they wouldn't accept it. Their grasshopper mentality kept them from the promises of God. God had taken them out of Egypt, but He couldn't take Egypt out of them. That was their responsibility. It was up to them to accept the Word of God and reject their old way of thinking. God confirmed His words through Moses with amazing miracles. But they didn't want to change. They were used to their stinky diapers. Their minds were focused on going back to the old life instead of pressing on to the new one. So they meditated on Satan's lies rather than on God's truth.

God had given the Israelites the truth that would set them free, but they still believed the lies that kept them in bondage. And because of their refusal to change, they all died in the wilderness. God used Caleb and Joshua to bring their children into the Promised Land forty years later, but that sad truth is that every Israelite forty years and older died in the wilderness because of old thoughts.

How many Christians hang on to the thoughts and attitudes of the world and never renew their minds to the Word of God? So many stay in their wilderness of depression, sin, stress, poverty or whatever problem may come along, and they never experience the Promised Land God has given them. Remember, John 10:10 says, **The thief does not come except to steal, and to kill, and to destroy. I have come that they may have life, and that they may have it more abundantly.**

Abundant life has been provided! But you must possess it. It won't fall on you like rain from the sky. Daily change is the life destined for every born-again Christian. If you aren't willing to change, renew your mind and go for it, you may live your whole life without receiving much of what God has provided for you. But if you are willing to change and begin renewing your mind, you can start living the abundant life God has provided for you!

STEPS TO PERSONAL TRANSFORMATION

1. _____ is the way of life.

   _____

2. Do I like change, or do I do what I can to avoid it?

   _____

   _____

3. What "promised lands" have I missed because of an unrenewed mind?

    _____

    _____

4. Are there parts of my past life that I hang on to or want to go back to?

    _____

    _____

5. How can I start moving into more of my "promised land" today?

    _____

    _____

7

The apostle John was an old man when he wrote one of the last letters to be included in the canon of Scripture. He had walked with Jesus since he was a young man. His revelations in the gospel of John cause us to realize the depth of his relationship and understanding of the Lord. It was after many years of Christian life that John wrote, **Beloved, I pray that you may prosper in all things and be in health, just as your soul prospers** (3 John 2).

John realized that the prosperity of our whole lives, including the health of our bodies, hinged on the condition of our souls. John understood that what is in us controls what comes out of us and ultimately produces life's experiences. The apostle is telling us that as our soul prospers, our life prospers.

So many Christians wonder about God's will when it comes to prosperity and health. It should be obvious to anyone who believes the Bible that John wouldn't pray a prayer that was contrary to the will of God. Neither would he have said that he prayed this prayer above every other prayer if it weren't so. If it weren't God's will for His people to prosper and live in health, the Holy Spirit would never have inspired John to believe it or record it as a part of holy Scripture.

The key to John's prayer in 3 John 2 is the *soul*. Theologians refer to the soul as the mind, emotions and will. There is much more to defining the soul, but three attributes are a good place to start:

- Your mind—reasoning and thinking processes
- Your emotions—feelings

- Your will—deciding and choosing processes

These things make up the soul and control, to a great degree, how you experience life. You will prosper and live in health even as your soul prospers, or you will struggle and be weak, even as your soul is weak.

RENEWING THE MIND KEY NUMBER 9:

YOUR SOUL, MIND, EMOTIONS AND WILL
MUST PROSPER BEFORE YOUR LIFE WILL PROSPER

The prophet Hosea said in chapter 4, verse 6 of his book, **My people are destroyed for lack of knowledge. Because you have rejected knowledge, I also will reject you from being priest for Me.**

Lack of knowledge devastates many Christians and holds them in a life of mediocrity. One of the greatest areas of confusion and lack of knowledge is in understanding the difference between the *soul* and *spirit*. Some teachers say they're both the same thing. Some say they're different but function together in harmony. While this is not a theological treatise, I do want to give some scriptural definitions of the soul and spirit, because it is crucial to living out the Word of God. If we don't know what the Lord is telling us to do, there is no way we can do it; and if we can't do it, we can be destroyed for lack of knowledge.

First Thessalonians 5:23 says, **Now may the God of peace Himself sanctify you completely; and may your whole spirit, soul, and body be preserved blameless at the coming of our Lord Jesus Christ.**

Paul is praying here that we be preserved "completely," or wholly—in every part of our beings. Then he lists each part of the human person: the spirit, soul and body. This verse illustrates the uniqueness of the spirit and the soul. Your spirit is sanctified, or made pure, when you are born again.

First Corinthians 6:17 says, **But he who is joined to the Lord is one spirit with Him.** But as we have seen, the ongoing sanctification of our lives takes place in the human soul and body, where the new birth doesn't produce change.

To continue our definition of the soul, let's look at Hebrews 4:12:

> **For the word of God is living and powerful, and sharper than any two-edged sword, piercing even to the division of soul and spirit, and of joints and marrow, and is a discerner of the thoughts and intents of the heart.**

Here we see that the Word is the final authority in all the issues of life. It alone will infallibly discern what is from the Lord (Spirit), and what is from man (soul). Only the Word is the final authority when judging the thoughts and intents of the heart of man. As we dissect this verse a bit more, I think you'll get some insight to the functions of the soul and spirit of man. Here's an idea of what this verse is saying:

Soul — Spirit

Joints — Marrow

Thoughts — Intents of the heart

By inspiration of the Holy Spirit, the writer of Hebrews relates man's *soul, joints* and *thoughts.* Your soul is a connector for your spirit and body. It brings the spiritual realm and the physical realm into relationship so you can live as a spiritual being in relation to God and function in a natural world. As you hear things in your spirit, which is born of the Holy Spirit, you also hear it in your soul. Sometimes you "just know." Sometimes you'll say, "Something told me," and you will feel as if the Holy Spirit has just spoken personally to you. This is the process of the soul's connecting the spirit and body as a joint.

Then we see that the soul is related to thoughts. This is the major tool and function of the soul. Your thoughts direct your decisions, actions and feelings every day. And your thoughts take place in your soul.

Notice also that the spirit of man is related to marrow and intents. Marrow is the life-giving force in the bones where blood is created. The Old Testament tells us that life is in the blood. (Lev. 17:11.) Intents are the deep desires and purposes of our hearts. Both of these things describe the spirit man.

If you understand that the soul is not the same as the spirit, you can see why it is possible to be a born-again Christian with a saved spirit but struggling in life because of an unrenewed soul. This is why in Romans 12:2 God tells every believer to **be transformed by the renewing of your mind.**

Though your spirit is saved, your soul must be saved as you renew your mind, emotions and will to the Word of God. To the degree that you do this determines the amount of prosperity and health you experience in life.

These truths enable us to understand Scriptures like Proverbs 23:7: **For as [a man] thinks in his heart, so is he.** And Matthew 22:37: **"You shall love the Lord your God with all your heart, with all your soul, and with all your mind."**

The habitual thoughts of our minds control how we live. So Jesus commands us to do more than just believe in God; He commands us to love Him with our hearts. He gets even more specific when He commands us to love Him with all our souls. Then He finally makes it crystal clear when He commands us to love Him with our minds. To love the Lord with *all* that is within us in our hearts and minds, we must remove every thought that is contrary to our loving Him.

RENEWING THE MIND KEY NUMBER 10:

THE SOUL AND SPIRIT OF MAN
MAKE UP THE HEART OF MAN

Did you note at the end of Hebrews 4:12 the phrase, *of the heart?* The spirit and soul make up the heart of man. At different times throughout the Scriptures, the word *heart* is used to describe the whole person or a particular part of the inner person.

Second Corinthians 4:16 says, **Even though our outward man is perishing, yet the inward man is being renewed day by day.** Now, let's reason together a little. Paul can't be talking about the human spirit, since it is born again when a Christian makes Jesus the Lord of his life. So he is saying that the inward man, which is made up of spirit and soul, is renewed as we walk with the Lord—even though the outward man, the physical body, is getting older and dying a bit every day.

Part of Christian growth is getting to a place where we can follow our spirits instead of our flesh. The flesh is constantly desiring worldly, carnal, negative things, but the spirit is joined to the Lord and desires only godly things. The soul hears the desires of both and can follow either the spirit or the flesh. Remember, the soul is the joint, or *connector.*

When your spirit says, "I want to pray for thirty minutes and seek the Lord this morning," but your flesh says, "I want to stay in bed and watch TV," your soul is the controller. And your soul must decide which one you're going to follow. The weak Christian will follow the flesh; the strong Christian will go with the leading of his spirit.

The reason God is so concerned with the sanctification or purifying and renewal of your soul is that without it, you will be constantly controlled by your fleshly desires.

A prosperous soul is one that hears and chooses to follow the spirit man. The Bible promises that as we do that, we will prosper and live in health in every realm of life. This prosperity is not an extravagant lust for money or material things. It is having your needs met and abundance enough to be a blessing to those around you.

RENEWING THE MIND KEY NUMBER 11:

THE PROSPEROUS SOUL HEARS AND AGREES WITH THE SPIRIT

Those who question their salvation experience and wonder if they are really saved are usually people who have weak souls and are controlled by their flesh. They struggle to live for the Lord but feel as if they can't obey the Spirit. Consequently they feel unsaved.

But as this type of Christian is strengthened through the Word of God and his soul begins to prosper, his whole life begins to prosper as he senses the Holy Spirit working in his spirit. Now, the Holy Spirit was there all the time, but that Christian couldn't follow Him because of the state of his soul.

Let's look at eight things that constitute a poor soul.

1. Having a lack of knowledge of the Bible. (Hosea 4:6.)

2. Being controlled by the desires of the flesh (for example, not being able to control your weight, spending habits or sexual lusts). (Rom. 8:5.)

3. Being weak, indecisive or double-minded. (James 1:8.)

4. Fantasizing on negativity and feeling unable to control your thoughts. (2 Cor. 10:4,5.)

5. Refusing to change, defending past behavior and making excuses for yourself. (Prov. 9:7-9.)

6. Spending all your time on natural, earthly, material things. (Col. 3:1,2.)

7. Allowing emotions to control your attitudes and behaviors. (Eph. 4:22-24.)

8. Allowing fear, anger, bitterness, gossip or negative thinking to consume you. (Phil. 4:8.)

RENEWING THE MIND KEY NUMBER 12:

THROUGH THE WORD OF GOD AND SINCERE EFFORT, THE POOR SOUL CAN BE MADE PROSPEROUS

Now let's look at eight elements of a *prosperous* soul:

1. Being hungry to learn and change. (Matt. 5:6.)

2. Having a mind that meditates God's Word and follows its precepts. (Psalm 1:1-3.)

3. Having a disciplined mind and will that agree with the Spirit. (Rom. 8:6.)

4. Focusing on godly thoughts and attitudes. (Matt. 6:33.)

5. Confessing your faults openly and seeking change. (James 5:16.)

6. Having a mind that is set on things that heaven and God are involved with. (Col. 3:1-10.)

7. Having control over feelings and emotions. (2 Cor. 5:17.)

8. Having a pure, positive, happy attitude towards life. (Phil. 4:8.)

Please take the time to read through every one of these Scriptures. Memorize the verses that particularly speak to you, and make them your devotional for as long as you need. Then work through the following steps of personal transformation and move into chapter 8 to discover the power of the truth.

STEPS TO PERSONAL TRANSFORMATION

1. I must prosper in my_____ before I will prosper in other realms of life.

2. My soul is made up of my_____ and _____.

3. My heart is made up of my_____ and _____.

4. How has my soul agreed with the flesh and brought defeat to a part of my life?

_____

_____

5. Of the eight things listed concerning a poor soul, what are the three main things that cause my soul to be poor?

_____

_____

_____

8

THE POWER OF THE TRUTH

The apostle John had walked with Jesus since he was a young man. For months he followed Jesus in the flesh and was a part of the Lord's most intimate experiences. He saw Jesus transformed on the mount with Moses and Elijah. He laid his head on the Lord's bosom during the Last Supper. And he went with the Lord into the Garden of Gethsemane.

So I'm sure you would agree that this old apostle knew the Lord and His ways on a very special level. And I want to look again at how in 3 John 2, John starts his letter by sharing a prayer that he prayed above every other:

Beloved, I pray that you may prosper in all things and be in health, just as your soul prospers.

This introduction and prayer of John's establishes several very important truths for the Christian. As I said before, we know that John wouldn't pray something that was contrary to the will of God. And even if he would have, the Holy Spirit wouldn't have it recorded and placed it in the canon of Scripture. So by inspiration of the Holy Spirit, John prays that we may prosper and live in health. This is God's truth, not tradition, so we must realize it as God's will for His people before we will actively search it out.

Someone once disparagingly called me a health-and-wealth preacher—although I actually teach all the subjects of the New Testament. When I thought about that accusation, I realized that it's a lot better to preach health and wealth than sickness and poverty. By misunderstanding the words of the apostle John and many other passages of Scripture, the church world has preached doctrines of sickness, poverty and defeat that have enabled the world to dominate the Church. These doctrines have kept many from entering the kingdom of God. But that's not God's will!

GOD CREATED YOU TO PROSPER AND BE HEALTHY— POVERTY AND SICKNESS ARE NOT HIS WILL

John goes on to explain how God's beloved are to prosper and live in health: **just as your soul prospers.**

All success in the Christian life starts on the inside of the person and flows out. Jesus said in Matthew 12:35, **"A good man out of the good treasure of his heart** [the spirit and soul] **brings forth good things, and an evil man out of the evil treasure brings forth evil things.**

When our souls prosper, we have good treasure, which we can bring forth. But when our souls are poor, or full of negative thoughts, attitudes and beliefs, we have evil treasure which will bring forth defeat, despair and problems.

When we buy into the lie that the things outside of us are controlling the outcome of our lives, we enter into bondage. So many people really believe that if the government were different, if their workers' union would do something or if their company would make a new policy, their lives would be successful. The fact is, although those outer things may have some minor influence on life, what is in you controls the kind of life you experience.

Outer circumstances may bring certain difficulties our way, so we must choose how to deal with those things. It is up to each individual either to rise above his circumstances or be defeated by them. When you have prosperity and health on the inside in your soul, you will bring it forth and see it manifested in every area of life.

In 3 John 3-4, John says, **For I rejoiced greatly when brethren came and testified of the truth that is in you, just as you walk in the truth. I have no greater joy than to hear that my children walk in truth.**

So the apostle tells us here that the foundation of having a prosperous soul is to walk in truth. He gave us the example of a group of Christians—the truth was in them, and they walked in it. There is a twofold insight here that I believe is very important for us to see.

The first insight is this: Truth is God's Word. Remember, Jesus said in John 8:31-32, **"If you continue in My word, then you are My disciples indeed. And you shall know the truth, and the truth shall make you free."**

In John 17:17 He said, **"Your word is truth."**

Only when we have heard, received and renewed our minds to the Word of God is the truth in us. This is the foundation for a prosperous soul. We must accept God's Word as the highest and the final authority. It is higher than religious traditions, church decrees, family and cultural traditions and every other order of life. God has exalted His Word even above His name. (Ps. 138:2.) Heaven and earth will pass away, but the Word of God will stand forever.

Proverbs 4:20-23 says:

My son, give attention to my words; incline your ear to my sayings. Do not let them depart from your eyes; keep them in the midst of your heart; for they are life to those who find them, and health to all their flesh. Keep your heart with all diligence, for out of it spring the issues of life.

In this passage, we see that the issues of life come not from outer circumstances but from the heart.

RENEWING THE MIND KEY NUMBER 14:

GOD'S WORD IS THE TRUTH— THE BASIS FOR ALL SUCCESS IN LIFE

The second insight in 3 John 3-4 is found in the definition of the Greek word we translate truth. The Greek is *aletheia,* and it literally means "nothing concealed."[1] It is appearance being reality. We could read this verse, "I have no greater joy than to hear that My children live with nothing concealed, walking in the reality of how they appear."

This is a greatly needed revelation in our world today, because most people live lies of deception and hypocrisy.

In America today, it is considered normal and even assumed that we will be phony, say what others want to hear and do whatever it takes to get what we want. The truth is meaningless as we break our marriage vows, leave our children, lie to the IRS and steal from our employer. But the Christian is called to have a prosperous soul, one that is filled with truth and walks in truth. We are to live openly and honestly before all men.

The hypocrite is one who acknowledges the Lord and goes to church but couldn't care less about godly living. The hypocrite is one who is in church and says amen to the preacher and acts like he loves the Lord— that is, until he gets to the car, where he cusses out his wife, puts the kids down and goes home to have a beer and watch the game. He's on the deacon board but seldom pays his whole tithes or follows through on his pledges. He acts nicely to the people he works with but gossips about them behind their backs.

The Greek word for *hypocrite* originally didn't have a negative connotation. It described the actors in a stage play who used different masks to play various characters. New Testament writers began to use the word to describe the phony or the person who hides and conceals the truth. Jesus called the religious leaders of His day hypocrites because they faked their dedication to God's Word and lived according to man-made traditions (much like many Christians today) in their daily lives.

The prosperous soul is open and honest. Nothing is concealed, and the face value is the real value. If we have truth in us and are walking in truth, there is a commitment and a passion in our lifestyle. Many Christians have a halfhearted commitment to truth, so they have a halfhearted walk and relationship with the Lord. They believe the Bible, but there are parts they don't want to deal with. They don't want to pray with the Spirit, lift up hands in worship, bind an evil spirit or give 10 percent of their income to their church. Many hide things from their wives or husbands, keeping feelings and things they've done concealed. They say they believe the truth, but they don't walk in it.

RENEWING THE MIND KEY NUMBER 15:

TO HAVE THE TRUTH IN US IS TO LIVE IT EVERY DAY

In Revelation 3:15-16 Jesus says He wants us to be hot or cold, not lukewarm. The lukewarm person will be spewed out.

I pray this stern rebuke is not seen as some kind of condemnation. It should be viewed rather as reproof and an opportunity to develop a prosperous soul and begin to prosper in all areas of your life. Because when the truth of God's Word and an honest, open lifestyle operate in your soul, you are on your way to the blessings of God.

Without God's Word and with things concealed in your life, you can never experience the prosperous soul. Every work that Satan is able to accomplish on earth is based on a lie. He is the father of all lies according to Jesus, and when he gets someone to believe a lie, he can do his evil work in and through them.

When society believes the lie that life isn't sacred, unborn babies, senior citizens and the terminally ill can be legally murdered.

When we believe that marriage, as another example, is not a divine institution, we can break our marriage vows, commit adultery and sleep with whomever we want.

Lies are the basis for every negative thing in our lives. When you doubt God's Word, you believe Satan's word.

God says He will meet all our needs according to His riches in glory, but we often worry because we don't see *how* our needs will be met. (Phil. 4:19.) So we believe a lie.

God says He will heal all our diseases, but most Christians believe what a doctor says more than what God says! Now, I don't mean we shouldn't go to doctors, but the point is, we need to get serious about the power of God's truth.

Through standing on the Word of God and living an honest lifestyle, we can be the kind of people the great apostle John rejoiced over. He had no greater joy than to see people have the truth in them as they walked in the truth. That is how they had a prosperous soul and every part of their lives prospered. And this is why you will have a prosperous soul—so every part of your life will prosper!

STEPS TO PERSONAL TRANSFORMATION

1. Do I believe God has created me to prosper and live in health?

   _____

2. What is the key to the prosperous soul in 3 John 2-3?

   _____

3. What areas of my life are hypocritical?

   _____

4. In what areas of my life do I know the truth but don't live it?

   _____

5. Is the truth of God's Word a valuable, foundational part of my life?

   _____

9

THE MIND: CONTROL
CENTER OF YOUR LIFE

The mind is an amazing and powerful creation of God. No animal has a mind like ours, no machine or computer can match its abilities and no human has tapped its full potential. It is the control center of our lives. It stores all experiences and learned material. It reasons and creates information; it chooses from a myriad of options every day. It plans and sees into the future with an imagination that is unlimited. It has been said that a mind is a terrible thing to waste, and yet we waste our minds daily. Even in the Christian world, we let our minds wander and lead us into mediocrity and negativity.

Romans 8:5-6 says:

> For those who live according to the flesh set their minds on the things of the flesh, but those who live according to the Spirit, the things of the Spirit. For to be carnally minded is death, but to be spiritually minded is life and peace.

God established the mind as a center of reasoning, deciding, believing and envisioning. This passage in Romans shows us that the mind decides whether we live in the flesh—which is the sin nature, negative desires and the lower unregenerate part of man—or in the spirit—the godly, holy, recreated part of the Christian. If we set our minds on negative desires, imaginations or experiences, we will eventually follow those thoughts and begin to practice some degree of them.

The things we set our minds on soon become behavior. It is well documented that what a child watches on TV affects his behavior. If it's a violent cartoon, he usually becomes agitated and aggressive. If it's, say, *Mr. Rogers,* he has a more mild and stable demeanor. Likewise, the man who watches pornographic movies will seek the sexual fantasies he has watched. I believe much of the rape, incest and sexual violence of our world can be traced to pornography.

God designed our minds to be great tools in learning His ways, not only while we are here on earth, but throughout eternity. We have the ability to grasp information and use it like no other creature. Like an iron trap, we create pictures and thoughts that stay with us our entire lives. God's plan is that humans would receive His Word and understand His ways in order to fellowship with Him on His level forever.

Adam was to receive all the knowledge he needed from the Father, not from evil or negative sources. The Tree of the Knowledge of Good and Evil was there to give Adam a choice—to learn from God or from the world. As long as he chose to receive God's Word, Adam prospered, and he would have continued to learn everything and more than the tree of knowledge could ever have given him. But by partaking of the knowledge or thoughts of the world, Adam opened his mind and spirit to things contrary to God.

The first effect of Adam's sin was spiritual death, or separation from God. Then came a way of life that eventually ended in physical death.

Through Jesus, we come back to God spiritually when we are born again. But our minds must be renewed by the knowledge of God if we are to walk with Him on a daily basis. The goal of every Christian should be to have the kind of relationship with the Lord that He originally planned in the beginning. Though we will never be back in the Garden with a born-again spirit *and* a renewed mind, we can walk with God again.

In Romans 8:5-6, which we read earlier, Paul says that what you set your mind on is the controlling factor between living a spiritual or carnal life. If we think on the things of the negative world around us, we will live carnal, negative, worldly lives. And Paul says the carnal mind brings death.

What kind of death is Paul speaking of? Spiritual death? No, because if that is so, most Christians have lost their salvation and are spiritually dead, since most have unrenewed minds. The kind of death he is speaking of is separation from the blessing and provision of God.

To be dead in its fullest sense is to be separated. To be *physically dead* is to be separated from your body. To be *spiritually dead* is to be separated from the eternal life of God.

But the kind of death that the carnal mind brings is illustrated in Luke 15 in the parable of the prodigal son. In this story Jesus speaks of an ungrateful son who left his father, wasted his inheritance on worldly living and finally found himself eating the hogs' food. His foolishness had separated him from his father's loving care, and he was miserable, trying to make a living in a negative world.

The Scripture says, **"And when he came to himself,"** the son went back to his father and repented of what he had done (v. 17). And when the father greeted him, he said, **"For this my son was dead and is alive again"** (v. 24). Then he hugged him, clothed him and restored him, celebrating his return with a great party.

Now, the son was never physically dead, nor did he ever stop being the man's son. But by leaving the father and following his own carnal thoughts, he was separated from, or dead to, the provision and the protection of the father. It took some heavy-hitting bottom living for this son to wake up. But he did and renewed his mind to come home.

RENEWING THE MIND KEY NUMBER 16:

WHERE YOU SET YOUR MIND WILL CONTROL WHERE YOU GO IN LIFE

Like the separated prodigal, many Christians today are dead to the protection and provision of God. They live as though they weren't children of the Father—with the same struggles and failures as those who don't know God. Many Christians even question their new-birth experience because they go through the same challenges as the world and think they can't really be saved.

There are those who have concluded that the whole Christian faith is just another religion because of the negative things that have happened to them. They figure that if God was real in their lives, certain things would not have happened to them. The problem is a lack of knowledge about the renewing of their minds. God is with them, and they really are His sons or daughters; but they are living in the "hog pens" of life because their minds are full of the thoughts of the world.

Now let me end the parallel of the prodigal here. Just because people live in the hog pens of life doesn't mean they seek after sin or evil. It means they are living in separation from the knowledge and will of God. They live constantly in fear and unbelief, and their minds have opened the door to negativity, separating them from the protection and provision of the Father.

The carnal mind is death—separation—but the spiritual mind is life and peace.

In the *Williams New Testament,* Romans 8:5-6 says:

People who live by the standard set by their lower nature are usually thinking the things suggested by that nature.... To be thinking things suggested by the lower nature means death. For to be thinking things suggested by the spirit means life and peace.

The focus of our minds is the issue Paul is dealing with here. When we focus on fleshly, sensual, greedy and materialistic desires or thoughts of anger, frustration and violence, we are cut off from the life and peace of God. Then we find ourselves living out our thoughts. But when we focus on the thoughts of God, the Word of God and the way God would have us live each day, we live out His thoughts and have His provision and protection.

Isaiah 26:3 says, **You will keep him in perfect peace, whose mind is stayed on You, because he trusts in You.** Now, that doesn't mean we walk around thinking about nothing but God all the time. He knows our minds are the control centers of our lives and that we must do our jobs and look after our households.

John 1:1 tells us, **The Word was God.** So when we think in line with the Word of God, when our attitudes are controlled by the Word of God, when we face life with the Word of God—that's what it actually means to have our minds stayed on Him.

Staying our minds on Him is how the life and peace of God become our life and peace. People are looking for peace through drugs, romance, material things, religion, New-Age philosophy and many other things, but they never find it. Peace only comes to those who have a spiritual mind which they focus on the Word of God, not allowing their flesh or the world to control them.

RENEWING THE MIND KEY NUMBER 17:

AS YOU REFOCUS YOUR MIND, YOU TAKE A NEW PICTURE OF YOUR FUTURE

When I began to learn about the difference between a carnal and a spiritual mind, I was a drug addict who had almost destroyed his life. My thoughts were so crazy that half the time I didn't know what I was thinking, and the other half I wanted no one else to know. Once I was born again, focusing my mind on positive things was nearly impossible. If God had not said I could do it, I wouldn't have tried.

Through months of diligent work in learning the Word and setting my mind on it, I began to get control of my thoughts and build a spiritual mind.

When I felt depressed, rather than having a drink or smoking a joint, I began to think on the destiny God planned for my life.

When I was angry and wanted to punch someone's lights out, I began to think about the great love that motivated Jesus to give His life for me.

When I started to worry about bills and money, I would stop and think about God's promises to meet all my needs and prosper my life. Soon I began to experience the peace of God, because my mind was stayed on Him. I began to see His provision and blessing, because I was following the things of the Spirit, not the things of the flesh. And the same can happen for you.

We must practice setting our minds on the things of God, not the things of the world, so that our control centers will direct us toward God. Meditation is simply thinking about something. We all meditate every day, all day. But the problem is, we often meditate on negative, selfish, fearful, worldly things. However, if we think on or meditate on the Word of God day and night, Psalm 1:3 says that we will be **like a tree planted by the rivers of water, that brings forth its fruit in its season, whose leaf also shall not wither; and whatever he does shall prosper.**

When you can control your mind, you can control your destiny, because the truth of God's Word is the basis for all success in life.

STEPS TO PERSONAL TRANSFORMATION

1. The control center of my life is the _____.

2. What things do I think about that produce negative results in my life?

   _____

   _____

3. What areas of my thinking are spiritual?

   _____

   _____

4. What areas of my thinking are carnal?

_____

_____

5. What would I like to focus my thoughts on to build a new future?

_____

_____

10

> For the weapons of our warfare are not carnal but mighty in
> God for pulling down strongholds, casting down arguments and
> every high thing that exalts itself against the knowledge of God,
> bringing every thought into captivity to the obedience of Christ.
>
> 2 Corinthians 10:4,5

Paul is showing us in this passage where the greatest warfare of the Christian life really takes place—the mind. Though we do have to deal with demon spirits, Jesus has already defeated them and has given us His victory. However, we still do have to fight for the victory over the negative thoughts that can fill our minds and control our lives. As we have already looked at briefly, Paul says there are "strongholds" that can take root in the human mind but which must be brought down.

Stronghold is a military term that describes a fortified place, or a place of domination and control. Through the input of parents, secular schools and the secular media, we all develop habits of thought that often contradict the Word of God. Some Christians have strongholds of fear and worry. Others have strongholds of anger and bitterness. Others have strongholds of sexual sin, greed, selfishness or laziness.

RENEWING THE MIND KEY NUMBER 18:

WE CAN CAPTURE EVERY THOUGHT AND BRING IT TO THE OBEDIENCE OF THE WORD OF GOD

The first step in dealing with negative thoughts is to become aware of them so we can "capture" them. To capture these thoughts is to reject them from our minds once we recognize them. Then we must submit them to the Word of God. By rejecting negative thoughts and focusing on the thoughts of God, we pull down these strongholds and drive them out. Of course, this is not an instantaneous change. It takes discipline and diligence, but it can be done.

When a born-again Christian recognizes the need for change, the role of the mind in changing and God's power to change, he can take control his life. Paul says in 2 Timothy 1:7, **For God has not given us a spirit of fear, but of power and of love and of a sound mind.**

We can have a sound, disciplined, strong mind, and we can think the thoughts of God, reason according to the Word of God and reject the thoughts of the world. The lack of a sound, disciplined mind is a major problem in many people's lives today. The evidence of that lack is glaring: the failure of public schools, the number of hours the average person watches TV, the decline of real leaders and the rise of welfare cases.

Most people don't exercise their minds. I once heard someone say, "Most people are on mental birth control pills." In other words, they don't produce successful lives! Most of our nation's young people are better Nintendo players than readers, people generally would rather watch someone on TV have an exciting life than to create one of their own and many high school graduates don't have even the basics for success in life. So we must get our minds in shape before we let our world sink deeper in failure.

RENEWING THE MIND KEY NUMBER 19:

GOD ENABLES US TO HAVE SOUND, DISCIPLINED MINDS

Nothing, including the mind, gets better on its own. Everything left to itself decays, loses power and declines. You don't have to work, for example, to get out of shape. That will just happen. But you have to work to get in shape and stay that way. You don't have to work to have a sloppy house—that comes naturally. But you have to work to keep things clean and sharp. In the same way, a lazy, negative mind comes naturally, but a sound, disciplined mind takes work. And it is worth working on, because the human mind left to itself will become stagnant, negative and sinful.

Jesus said,

> **"What comes out of a man, that defiles a man. For from within, out of the heart of men, proceed evil thoughts, adulteries, fornications, murders, thefts, covetousness, wickedness, deceit, licentiousness, an evil eye, blasphemy, pride, foolishness. All these evil things come from within and defile a man."**
>
> **Mark 7:20-23**

So we can't blame the devil when it's really our thoughts that open the door for evil and failure in our lives. If we don't strive to develop a sound mind, the things Jesus spoke of will begin to consume our minds.

Much of society today won't watch a movie or listen to a song that doesn't have sexual messages and evil overtones. Adultery is advised by many psychiatrists. Homosexuality is lauded, and fornication is expected, even among junior high kids. Horror movies, which are full of fear, hate and murder, are some of the most popular at the box office. Rather than pull down the strongholds in our minds and capture the thoughts that destroy us, we would rather go with what is socially acceptable, with what is "cool." Mark 7:20 in *The Living Bible* says, **It is the thought life that pollutes.**

The key to pulling down strongholds, capturing every thought and developing a sound mind is found in Joshua 1:8:

> **This Book of the Law shall not depart from your mouth, but you shall meditate in it day and night, that you may observe to do according to all that is written in it. For then you will make your way prosperous, and then you will have good success.**

In this passage, Joshua was taking over leadership of the nation of Israel, who were just preparing to possess their Promised Land. He had a very difficult position, and God was giving him the key to his success as a leader. Joshua was to keep God's Word in his mouth and in his mind. If he did this, God promised him prosperity and good success. By the same token, we understand that if he filled his mouth full of fearful and negative words or he filled his mind with worry and worldly thinking, he would fail and not possess the promises of God.

RENEWING THE MIND KEY NUMBER 20:

WE ALL MEDITATE EVERY DAY, BUT WHAT ARE WE MEDITATING ON?

Though most people don't realize it, we all meditate day and night. *Meditation* is simply thinking about something. The Hebrew word means to think on, ponder, mutter to oneself or picture in the mind.[1] It is impossible to think about nothing, so we meditate all our waking hours. The question is, what are you meditating on? Is your mind focused on the things of God and His way of dealing with the issues you are facing? Or are you thinking on thoughts of anger, frustration, bitterness, anxiety and so forth? God says the things you meditate on will decide whether you prosper and have good success or struggle through life just trying to make a living.

I want you to read Psalm 1:1-3 once more, because it gives us insight into the benefits of controlling our thoughts, and the benefits of meditating on God's Word:

> **Blessed is the man who walks not in the counsel of the ungodly, nor stands in the path of sinners, nor sits in the seat of the scornful; but his delight is in the law of the Lord, and in His law he meditates day and night. He shall be like a tree planted by the rivers of water, that brings forth its fruit in its season, whose leaf also shall not wither; and whatever he does shall prosper.**

Once again, we see the importance of keeping our thoughts on the right things and what the positive outcome of doing so will bring.

So many Christians think the reason they are poor and suffering is that God's will is for them to suffer—when in fact, they suffer because of their negative mentality. They think on small, poverty-stricken, mediocre things, and that's what they have in life. If they would fill their thoughts with the Word of God, they would be like a fruitful tree that brings forth fruit and their lives would begin to prosper in every way. Prosperity doesn't necessarily mean money, although money is a part of it. Prosperity includes marriage, family, relationships, church life, career and health. God wants every part of Christians' lives to prosper. But the mind is the control center, so it must be programmed right.

Notice that the Psalmist cautioned about whom we walk through life with and where we receive counsel from. Proverbs tells us that we become like the people we hang around. (Prov. 13:20.) It is pretty obvious that you won't grow beyond the level of people you spend the most time with. Look around at those closest to you. That is a picture of where you are or where you are going. If you like what you see, great. But if you don't want to live like those you hang around most, if you want to continue to move forward in life, you will have to get some new friends.

Mom and Dad may not be the best source for counsel. Remember, their counsel will only take you as far as they have gone and no further. If they've never been where you're trying to go, they probably can't help you get there. If you listen to the ungodly, the sinner or the scornful, the Psalmist says you will not be blessed. In other words, negative relationships bring a curse.

It is next to impossible to meditate on the things of God and fellowship with worldly people. I'm not advocating that we hide from the world, but I do think we need to watch whom we allow to influence our lives. We want to be an influence on people around us. So for that reason, we will have relationships with those who need the Lord. But we must not allow them to pull us down to their level of negativity and hinder our walk with God.

You may be in a situation with an unsaved spouse or are still living at home with unsaved parents. In these cases, you can't leave the person. But you must guard your mind to keep your thoughts right and avoid allowing the negative environment to control or drag you down. When you can get around others who are like-minded it is important. I call this principle "hanging out with yourself" in our final chapter.

RENEWING THE MIND KEY NUMBER 21:

YOU MAY HAVE TO BUILD NEW FRIENDSHIPS BEFORE YOU CAN RENEW YOUR MIND

When a computer or a machine is programmed correctly, it gives the proper information and does the job it was created to do. In the same way, when the mind is programmed correctly, when it is renewed with the Word of God and stays focused on it, our lives will prosper as we accomplish the things God created us to accomplish.

You weren't created to struggle through life and barely make it. God said you can take dominion, prosper and have good success. But you must take control. As you control your mind, you control your life; you will prosper and live in health, even as your soul prospers.

STEPS TO PERSONAL TRANSFORMATION

1. What three problems in my life may be strongholds in my mind?

  _____

  _____

  _____

2. What do I meditate on more than anything else?

   _____

   _____

3. How could I meditate on God's Word more?

   _____

   _____

4. Where do I receive most of my counsel from?

   _____

   _____

5. Which friends do I have who will help me renew my mind? Which friends have been hindering me?

   _____

   _____

11

THE GREAT EXCHANGE

And do not be conformed to this world, but be transformed by the renewing of your mind, that you may prove what is that good and acceptable and perfect will of God.

Romans 12:2

A s we established earlier, to be transformed is to be changed in form, become completely different, go through a metamorphosis or exchange one form for another. A caterpillar goes through a transformation that causes it to become something different than it was. Once transformed it no longer crawls on branches and leaves; it flies through the air. It no longer has a long, fuzzy body; it is a beautiful butterfly.

This is the kind of change God wants in our lives. When we come to Him, it's not so we can join a religion or have something to do on Sunday mornings. No, we can actually become a new species of beings— new creations, as Paul said in 2 Corinthians 5:17: **Therefore, if anyone is in Christ, he is a new creation; old things have passed away; behold, all things have become new.**

Of course, these aren't physical changes. Spiritual and mental changes occur as we renew our minds to the Word of God. The transformation of our minds causes us to be different than those in the world. We have a new way of thinking, a new way of acting, a new outlook on life, a new strength and power. We no longer go through the same troubles and despair. When problems do come, we face them with the Word and the Spirit of God, and we overcome them rather than being overcome by them.

Renewing the Mind Key Number 22:

We Can Exchange Our Lack for God's Abundance

The transforming change that God desires to do in His children starts in our spirits when we are born again. The change, however, must continue in the soul realm if we are going to accomplish all that God has for us. Notice that Romans 12:2 says we reach the *perfect* will of God only as we renew our minds.

Paul also says in Colossians 3:1-5,9-10:

> If then you were raised with Christ, seek those things which are above, where Christ is, sitting at the right hand of God. Set your mind on things above, not on things on the earth. For you died, and your life is hidden with Christ in God. When Christ who is our life appears, then you also will appear with Him in glory.
>
> Therefore put to death your members which are on the earth: fornication, uncleanness, passion, evil desire, and covetousness, which is idolatry.... Do not lie to one another, since you have put off the old man with his deeds, and have put on the new man who is renewed in knowledge according to the image of Him who created him.

In this passage, Paul is describing a great exchange of the carnal mind's futile way of thinking for God's way of thinking. This great exchange involves, as Paul says, putting off the old man and putting on the new man which is renewed in the knowledge of God. We give up the old way and receive a whole new way of living. We leave the kingdom of the devil and enter into the kingdom of God. We exchange our old way of thinking and acting for a new way. We exchange our lack for God's abundance.

Paul says this new man is recreated according to the image of Christ: **For whom He foreknew, He also predestined to be conformed to the** image of His Son, that He might be the firstborn among many brethren (Rom. 8:29).

As we exchange our ways for His, we begin to experience this higher level of life that Paul is talking about. We are no longer controlled by the thoughts, attitudes, desires and actions of the world, but we rise up to a new controlling source—the Spirit and Word of God.

Isaiah 55:7-9 says:

"Let the wicked forsake his way, and the unrighteous man his thoughts; let him return to the Lord, and He will have mercy on him; and to our God, for He will abundantly pardon. For my thoughts are not your thoughts, nor are your ways My ways," says the Lord. "For as the heavens are higher than the earth, so are My ways higher than your ways, and My thoughts than your thoughts."

The Lord is telling us that as we forsake our old thoughts and ways in exchange for His, we can live a higher level of life. But to experience God's ways, we must renew our minds with God's thoughts.

RENEWING THE MIND KEY NUMBER 23:

AS WE RENEW OUR MINDS WITH GOD'S HIGHER THOUGHTS, WE BEGIN TO EXPERIENCE GOD'S HIGHER WAYS

Verse after verse in the Word of God tells us that if we want to reprogram our minds according to God's thoughts, we must renew our minds to His Word. As we do so, we begin to rise up to His higher life. This is the great exchange. We give Him our low life and get His high life. We give our death and get His life. We give our sin and get His righteousness. We give our sickness and get His healing. We give our poverty and get His prosperity. As we let go of what is ours in the natural realm of life, we receive what is His in the supernatural.

Jesus put the great exchange this way: **Whoever finds his [lower] life will lose it [the higher life], and whoever loses his [lower] life on My account will find it [the higher life]** (Matt. 10:39 AMP).

So many people are afraid to let go of what is theirs in order to receive what is His. They know that what they have isn't much, but it's all they've got. So they hang on to it. Although that thing does not give them the life they want, they hang on to it.

The alcoholic hates his booze but won't give it up.

The poor person hates his poverty but won't change the lifestyle that keeps him poor.

The overweight person hates the fat but won't do what it takes to get fit.

The lazy person hates the feeling of dissatisfaction with life but won't give up his TV to make something happen.

People hang on to the carnal low life and give up God's higher life daily. Jesus said you have to get rid of the old wineskin before you can receive the new wine. Sometimes we hang on to the low, even though we know God's higher is better. We're tired of the old wine, but we're not ready to go for the new. So there must be a point in life where you aren't only tired of the old, but you are also ready to do *whatever it takes* to have the new.

RENEWING THE MIND KEY NUMBER 24:

ONLY WHEN YOU LET GO OF THE LOW LIFE WILL YOU LIVE THE HIGH LIFE

If you're through with your low life and want God's high life, then you'll get to a place where you will make the exchange, whatever the cost. You'll sell all, burn your bridges, abandon yourself and go for it! At this point, you are in the process of proving the perfect will of God and seeing the destiny God has for you. It is risky, it is scary and it is a new territory. But it is the most exciting and rewarding steps you will ever take in life.

When I moved into the drug rehabilitation center and began to build a new life, I left every old friend, every old habit and even my family for a time to start a new life for myself. I had to lose the low life before I could find the high life. It certainly wasn't easy, but it was the greatest exchange I have ever made.

Today I am moving on with God and making that exchange every day, and I plan to keep doing so for the rest of my life. I haven't arrived, I'll never be done and I never want to quit. And I hope by now, you are inspired to make the great exchange too!

STEPS TO PERSONAL TRANSFORMATION

1. How does transformation take place according to Romans 12:2?

   _____

   _____

2. Change starts in the _____ but must continue in the soul or _____ realm.

3. What specific thoughts of God have caused my life to rise up to a higher level?

   _____

   _____

4. What parts of the old man or low life have I hung on to that have stopped growth and change?

   _____

   _____

5. How do I feel about the risk of exchanging what I have for what God has?

_____

_____

12

We must have God's perspective on five areas if we are to move forward beyond conversion in our Christian walk. These are areas in which many people have little knowledge of the truth according to God's Word, and consequently, they struggle through life, living far out of the perfect will of God.

My desire in discussing these areas is to stir your thoughts about them. I invite you to seek after greater knowledge and insight in each area, because they are foundational to your success in the Lord and in life.

WE MUST BELIEVE THAT GOD HAS A PLAN AND A DESTINY FOR OUR LIVES

Most people in our world today live life simply to get by. They have no sense of purpose or destiny. Paying the monthly bills and getting a new car or maybe a bigger house is about all the destiny they think about. But the fact of the matter is that before God made the earth, He knew you and planned a great life for you. The average Christian never fulfills the destiny of God because he knows nothing about it and he lives for lower goals and desires.

Ephesians 1:3-6 says:

Blessed be the God and Father of our Lord Jesus Christ, who has blessed us with every spiritual blessing in the heavenly places in Christ, just as *He chose us in Him before the foundation of the world,* that we should be holy and without blame before Him in love, *having predestined us* to adoption as sons by Jesus Christ to Himself, according to the good pleasure of His will.

Ephesians 1:11 tells us we're *being predestined* according to the *purpose* of Him who works all things according to the counsel of His will.

Ephesians 2:10 (AMP) also sheds some light: **For we are God's [own] handiwork (His workmanship), recreated in Christ Jesus, [born anew] that we may do those good works which God predestined (planned beforehand) for us.**

God's predestination, according to what we read in Romans 8:29, is always based on His foreknowledge: **For whom He foreknew, He also predestined.**

All of these verses tell you that you aren't some puppet on a string with no choice in life. In fact, before the foundation of the world God gave you a will and then looked down through history to see the choices you would make. Based on His foreknowledge of your choices, He planned a fulfilling, rewarding, satisfying life for you.

So our greatest mission in life is not to establish our own dreams and work until they come to pass; but our mission is to seek God, find His plan and purpose for our lives and then go for it with all that is within us.

Most people in this world are unhappy going to work every day, because they don't feel they are fulfilling any purpose or destiny. Many try to do things they weren't called to do, and they merely emulate or try to be like someone else. Whether you are to teach, raise children, pastor a church or build airplanes, God has a great plan for your life that will offer the maximum fulfillment you can experience on earth.

Here are eight steps to discovering your destiny in the Lord:

1. Think about the real desire of your heart, not what someone else wants you to do or the fleeting fantasies of your mind. (Ps. 37:3-4.)

2. Determine what stirs your passion, drive and zeal. (John 2:17.)

3. Know what gifts and talents flow naturally through you. (Rom. 12:4-6.)

4. Seek counsel from mature Christian friends and leaders. (Prov. 11:14; 18:1.)

5. Listen to the witness of the Holy Spirit in your spirit. (Rom. 8:14.)

6. Understand what you can or can't give yourself to 100 percent in order to accomplish it. (1 John 3:16.)

7. Know what produces good fruit in your life. (Matt. 12:33.)

8. Follow the peace of God inside you. (Col.3:15.)

WE MUST BELIEVE THAT WHAT'S INSIDE US— NOT CIRCUMSTANCES OUTSIDE US—CONTROLS OUR LIVES

Now, it's easy for anyone to blame the government, society, family or events for the way we are today. Most people will agree with you when you begin to complain about the things around you that you think are controlling your life—whether it's the traffic that made you mad, the government who took your money, the boss who did you wrong or the spouse who keeps you upset. In reality, you are making choices about all these things. Your involvement with them and how you deal with them is determined by you.

While there are accidents and situations that we don't choose or want, the fact is, outside circumstances don't control our lives—we do.

It is easy to let the negative things that happen become the controlling factors in our lives, but we don't have to. We can rise up, take control of our thoughts and feelings and go on.

For example, when two of my close friends lost a two-month-old baby to Sudden Infant Death Syndrome, they had to decide how to deal with it. It devastated their lives—and mine—for a time. But they eventually rose up in faith and love and went on to minister to others according to the ultimate plan God destined for them. They didn't allow that tragedy to control them and throw them into a life of bitterness, anger or doubt.

Jesus said in Matthew 12:35, "**A good man out of the good treasure of his heart brings forth good things, and an evil man out of the evil treasure brings forth evil things.**"

It's not what's around you that controls your future; it's what's in you. In fact, your future is in your heart.

WE MUST BELIEVE THAT IF WE GIVE THE BEST, WE WILL HAVE THE BEST

Regardless of the economy or marketplace, God is a God of abundance. He told Abraham, "I am El Shaddai," the God who is more than enough. Abraham became a very rich man as he walked with God. (Gen. 12-17.) His riches weren't only in finances. Abraham prospered in his family, his other relationships and his spirituality. His son Isaac prospered in a land of famine and recession as he walked with God and obeyed His Word.

Jesus said in John 10:10, "**I have come that they may have life, and that they may have it more abundantly.**"

In Luke 6:38 we're told:

"**Give, and it will be given to you: good measure, pressed down, shaken together, and running over will be put into your bosom. For with the same measure that you use, it will be measured back to you.**"

The prophet Malachi tells us to bring our tithes, a tenth of our income, into the Church so there will be food in God's house. When we believe this promise is connected to our destiny and do it, the Lord can open the windows of heaven to pour out a blessing on us.

God wants mankind to enjoy His creation, including all the good things He has put on the earth. Nice things aren't here for Satan's people to enhance their lives of sin. The best properties weren't created for taverns or casinos; they are for the people of God to do the work of God and enjoy their relationship with Him. God didn't put Adam and Eve in a desert; He put them in a beautiful garden because He wanted them to be blessed.

As we renew our minds according to the Word of God and live according to His principles, we will see His abundance spiritually, mentally, physically and financially. We do not live for the blessings; we live for God, and as we live for Him, His abundant life and blessings are ours.

WE MUST ORDER OUR LIVES IN A BALANCED WAY AND KEEP OUR PRIORITIES IN LINE WITH GOD'S WILL

If your job takes priority over your family, you will soon lose your family, as many in our nation have already found. Over half of America's marriages are failing, and the main reason is wrong priorities in one or both spouses. When you put the wrong things first in life, you fail. There is no way around the reality of right priorities.

I heard one of our nation's top business speakers and consultants teach that you can't take time for your family *and* do all that is necessary to get ahead in business. Many buy into that philosophy and sacrifice their families, health and peace of mind.

It may be true that without the Lord, you can't prosper without giving everything else up. But with God, you can! If you will make Jesus the top priority of your life, He will enable you to succeed in business, family and every other area of your life. Jesus said, **"Seek first the kingdom of God and His righteousness, and all these things will be added to you"** (Matt. 6:33).

As you will discover, I like simple ways of looking at the complex issues of life. So here are six Fs to help you examine and schedule your priorities:

FAITH: Relationship with the Lord through regular prayer, Bible study and church attendance.

FITNESS: Mental and physical health through renewing the mind, study, regular exercise, proper rest and proper diet.

FAMILY: Strong, happy relationships with spouse and children through daily communication and time together.

FELLOWSHIP: Healthy relationships with friends who build you up and help you move toward your goals in life.

FINANCES: A fulfilling career that brings prosperity and fulfills your dreams.

FUN: Recreation and activities that enable you to enjoy the blessings you have received.

WE MUST BE EXCELLENT!

Excellence is key to experiencing God's will in every realm of life. But we live in a world where just getting by is viewed as good. We must realize that according to God's perspective, *good* is the enemy of *best*. Many people don't do their best on the job; they just do enough to get by. The problem is, they don't realize that there is more to being paid than the check they receive. New opportunities from the Lord, increases and prosperity come to those who are faithful in what is least. If you give your best, when nobody but God is looking, you will soon be faithful in much as well. (Luke 16:10-12.)

Daniel was a prophet in the Old Testament who was taken captive in Babylon as a young boy. His family was killed and his nation destroyed. He was a refugee in a great city with no family or people to help him. Now, Babylon was a New-Age, secular-humanist, demonic place that didn't serve God in any way. But in spite of all the things against him, Daniel rose up to be a leader in that nation and influenced many people.

Inasmuch as an excellent spirit, knowledge, understanding, interpreting dreams, solving riddles, and explaining enigmas were found in this Daniel.

Daniel 5:12

Because of his excellent spirit, Daniel was called upon and respected by the leaders of Babylon. If we Christians would get rid of that "barely get by" attitude and begin to go for excellence in every area of life, then we, too, could have a highly respected influence on our nation.

Mediocrity is a curse that causes people, families, businesses and ministries to exist far below their potential. It is only through excellence that we reach the height of our abilities. Because mediocrity is the norm in society and so much easier to attain, we must fight for excellence. It must be a drive and a passion that gets us up earlier in the morning, causes us to work longer at night and motivates us to give more than is required.

Psalm 8:1 says, **O Lord, our Lord,** *how excellent is Your name* **in all the earth, You who set Your glory above the heavens!** God's name describes His very being. So when He says His name is excellent, He is telling us that His character, nature, being and everything about Him are excellent. God isn't involved with mediocrity and lukewarmness. He goes for the best every time and is always excellent.

That's why the body of Christ must likewise strive for excellence. We must start where we are at and use whatever means we have. But the point is, we should always strive to improve and set our sights on excellence. You may not be there now (I know I'm not), but you're on the way. Don't accept a mediocre life. Fight for excellence in everything.

- Be excellent in your work.

- Be excellent in your parenting

- Be excellent in your relationships and communication.

- Be excellent in your home.

- Be excellent in your spirituality.

- Be an excellent person!

People achieving excellence always strive for improvement, and they learn to love change. You see, when you learn to love the transformation process—and the five areas in which your mind must be renewed—you will change!

STEPS TO PERSONAL TRANSFORMATION

1. Do I believe God has a plan for my life?

   _____

   _____

2. What parts of God's plan am I aware of at this point in my life?

   _____

   _____

3. What outside circumstances do I allow to control my life?

   _____

   _____

4. Am I willing to give the best to God that I might receive the best?

   _____

   _____

5. What priorities in my life are out of balance?

   _____

   _____

13

If we are to succeed in life, change and growth must become something we love, not just something we endure. If it is always a struggle to confront the truth, we will look for ways to avoid it. But when we fall in love with the truth and the results it produces in our lives, we will seek for it and always move forward in the Lord.

It's like the runner who finds that place of ecstasy—a "second wind"—as he runs. At first running is a labor and a discipline, but then he suddenly comes a place where he feels like he's floating. He's beyond having to force each step; his legs move effortlessly, and he enjoys the miles that drift by.

While just like physical exercise, change and growth will never be effortless, there is a place where it ceases to be a forced discipline and struggle.

Proverbs 9:7-9 talks about the person who despises change and the person who loves it:

> He who corrects a scoffer gets shame for himself, and he who rebukes a wicked man only harms himself. Do not correct a scoffer, lest he hate you; *rebuke a wise man, and he will love you.* Give instruction to a wise man, and he will be still wiser; *teach a just man, and he will increase in learning.*

Those who are scoffers, who have rebellious, stagnant spirits, will always react negatively when confronted with truth. They don't want to change and don't have the self esteem to look at their faults. So they hate the one who tells them the truth. You can examine yourself in this area by asking yourself, "Do I love the people who challenge me to change, or do I dislike and avoid them?"

RENEWING THE MIND KEY NUMBER 25:

THE BIGGEST CHANGE YOU MAY HAVE TO
MAKE IS WHOM YOU SPEND YOUR TIME WITH

Most people build a circle of friends who help them stay where they are in life without making any changes. They endorse each other's complacency. If one person tries to break out of the rut, the others pressure them not to move on so they won't be left behind. There is a kind of group pressure that stops growth.

But to renew the mind and go on in life, you must leave friends like these and develop new relationships. A real friend won't slow you down; he or she will help you grow and go on in life. Anyone who isn't helping you fulfill your destiny is hurting you. According to those verses in Proverbs, if you are wise, you will love the one who rebukes you. But if you are a fool, you will hate your rebuker.

Even the people closest to you—like parents—sometimes can be the most detrimental to your future. They subconsciously want to hold you where they are and keep you from growing. Without realizing it, they feel threatened if you move on, so they try to stop you.

Proverbs 13:20 says, **He who walks with wise men will be wise, but the companion of fools will be destroyed.** I can't say this enough: Check out who you are walking with and spending most of your time with. Changing companions may be the next change you need to make.

Proverbs 12:1 says, **Whoever loves instruction loves knowledge, but he who hates correction is stupid.** The wisdom of God in this verse tells us that we must decide to love the process of change, although it may not feel good at the time. If we avoid and despise it, we will become foolish and stupid. It's kind of like exercise; it may not feel enjoyable while you're sweating, but when your clothes fit well and your waist isn't hanging over your belt, you're glad you went through the pain.

The world exalts the rebellious and independent person. While there are positive aspects to being unique and nonconformist, God says, **Rebellion is as the sin of witchcraft, and stubbornness is as iniquity and idolatry** (1 Sam. 15:23). So when we resist change and growth, we actually open ourselves up to evil spirits and bring all kinds of negativity into our lives. Christians who refuse to flow with the Spirit of God and settle into a religious rut become some of the most rebellious, bigoted and stubborn people ever. The greatest hate and prejudice often come from religious people.

RENEWING THE MIND KEY NUMBER 26:

TO MAKE GROWTH AND CHANGE A PART
OF YOUR LIFESTYLE, YOU MUST LOVE IT

The wise in heart will receive commands, but a prating fool will fall.... The way of a fool is right in his own eyes, but he who heeds counsel is wise.

Proverbs 10:8; 12:15

We all want to be right, but the fact is, we are never right all the time. Rather than seeking to be corrected when we are wrong, human nature hides, denies and defends itself. I know many people who would rather fail at whatever they are doing than admit they had made a mistake. But the wise man who understands and submits to the maturity of correction will seek the Lord's counsel.

The following is a list of Proverbs that teach us to love change and correction. I invite you to memorize them and meditate on them as a part of the process of your mind renewal.

For the commandment is a lamp, and the law is light; reproofs of instruction are the way of life.

Proverbs 6:23

135

He who corrects a scoffer gets shame for himself, and he who rebukes a wicked man only harms himself. Do not correct a scoffer, lest he hate you; rebuke a wise man, and he will love you. Give instruction to a wise man, and he will be still wiser; teach a just man, and he will increase in learning.

Proverbs 9:7-9

Where there is no counsel, the people fall; but in the multitude of counselors there is safety.

Proverbs 11:14

A wise son heeds his father's instruction, but a scoffer does not listen to rebuke.

Proverbs 13:1

Poverty and shame will come to him who disdains correction, but he who regards a rebukewill be honored.... He who walks with wise men will be wise, but the companion of fools will be destroyed.

Proverbs 13:18,20

Harsh discipline is for him who forsakes the way, and he who hates correction will die.... A scoffer does not love one who corrects him, nor will he go to the wise.... Without counsel, plans go awry, but in the multitude of counselors they are established.

Proverbs 15:10,12,22

The ear that hears the rebukes of life will abide among the wise. He who disdains instruction despises his own soul, but he who heeds rebuke gets understanding. The fear of the Lord is the instruction of wisdom, and before honor is humility.

Proverbs 15:31-33

Never forget that when you follow the wisdom of God, you will prosper. But if you refuse to listen and grow, you will fail. So learn to love change!

STEPS TO PERSONAL TRANSFORMATION

1. What must I change in order to love the process of change?

_____

_____

2. Do any of my friends bring pressures that hinder me from changing?

_____

_____

3. What does Proverbs 9:7-9 tell me about receiving instruction?

_____

_____

4. How do I apply Proverbs 11:14 to the decisions I make?

_____

_____

5. Do I love the ones who correct me?

_____

_____

14

THERE ARE NO QUICK FIXES!

If you've made it this far in this book, you must have a real desire for change in your life. This is obviously not the most thrilling, exciting, spine-tingling message that can be studied. I have often wished—momentarily—that the Lord would have allowed me to emphasize healing, prosperity, miracles or the ministry of the Holy Spirit. But no, I'm called to teach on renewing the mind. This is certainly not a spontaneous, miraculous kind of teaching. But it does have deep and lasting effects.

In today's world, we like things quick and easy. If God would supernaturally remove all problems, attitudes and sin, we would all line up to have Him "get it together" for us. Most people are looking for that quick fix that will make their lives better. Whether it's finances, weight loss, building relationships or breaking bad habits—if there is a pill, a program or an easy way, we'll go for it.

We live in a "microwave" world. We want it quick and easy. America's present quick-fix thinking goes something like this:

Let's not wait for a solid relationship to grow; let's have sex now! Why get married? We'll just live together.

Solving problems is too hard; let's just get divorced!

Proper diet and exercise take too long! I need a pill.

Saving money is hard work. I need another credit card.

Children are too much responsibility. I'm having an abortion.

I could go on and on citing many other thoughts that prevail in our world about taking the easy way. The sad truth is that this same attitude prevails in the Church. As I said, if God would do a miracle, every Christian would line up for change. But if it takes discipline, effort and renewing of the mind, forget it!

RENEWING THE MIND KEY NUMBER 27:

MOST PEOPLE SPEND THEIR ADULT YEARS DEFENDING WHAT THEY KNOW, RATHER THANK SEEKING TO GROW

Most Christians don't grow spiritually after their first year or so in the Lord. It's not that they don't love God or that they don't want to go on with God. It's that they were raised to think that learning, growing and changing stop when you get out of high school or college. Then they spend the rest of their lives defending what they know, rather than seeking to grow.

Our present generation hasn't accepted the fact that our grandparents had some truth that we've let slip away. The previous generation knew that good things take time. A well-cooked meal, a well-built house or a loving relationship can't be made in a microwave. Life was slower for them, so quality and endurance were more common. It wasn't so important to get everything as quickly and easily as possible. Good things were worth the wait and the work to get them. I hope this isn't coming across as some "remember the good ol' days message," but we really have lost some of the values that our grandparents had.

Until 1945, the United States had no national debt, and if there were any, taxes were at a minimum. But then we slipped into the age of fast factory-built merchandise, fast marriages and even faster divorces, fast financial profits and losses, fast credit and fast foods.

While some of these things are fine, the overall effect on the nation has been devastating. We may never pay off the national debt. The average person leaves their children an inheritance of lack and shortage. Over half of today's marriages fail. Abortion kills thousands of children daily, and sexually transmitted diseases touch nearly every family in some way. The get-it-quick-and-easy life has brought pain, poverty and despair to our world.

In the Church, this quick-fix mentality has translated into an attitude of being spiritually lukewarm and mediocre. Many churches condone the worldly lifestyles of their members rather than teaching them to live in holiness. Some leaders give them the philosophy it takes but don't challenge them to change and grow. Much of the body of Christ has sacrificed the teaching and preaching of the Word of God for the religion and entertainment that attract the masses.

As a pastor, I know that it's one thing to have a crowd but it's an entirely different thing to have a church. There are many church attendees but few real members. But Psalm 92:13 says, **Those who are planted in the house of the Lord shall flourish in the courts of our God.** The solid, long-term, committed Christian is the one who sees the real blessings of the Lord. The "quick and easy" Christian never does.

If you are going to receive all that God has for you, you must follow His plan daily. Growth doesn't come with the laying on of hands from the pastor or the miraculous moving of the Spirit. Growth comes from renewing the mind according to the Word of God and practicing living that Word every day.

Long-term change through the renewing of the mind is the master key to all Christian growth. As we give ourselves to continued change and growth, we develop a flow in life that keeps us free from the negativity of stagnation. And we continually move forward in the will of God. Jesus said we must *continue* in His Word before we can know the truth. But then He said that the truth will set us free. Those who want a quick fix and don't continue in the truth never see freedom.

STEPS TO PERSONAL TRANSFORMATION

1. What things have I done in the quick and easy way that didn't produce good results?

   _____

   _____

2. What things do I defend that may be hindering my life?

   _____

   _____

3. Am I planted in a local church?

   _____

   _____

4. Am I involved with the Word of God or just religious activities?

   _____

   _____

5. Do I value the truth of God's Word and continue in it?

   _____

   _____

15

Many Christians drift and stagnate in life simply because they have no spiritual goals and never decide to press further. Many people begin a lifestyle of change, but they often abandon staying the course until significant transformation takes place because of distractions and lack of vision. Others aren't even sure real spiritual change is possible, so they take the carnal way and sit by the side of the road, never looking down the road to see where it leads.

Once a believer decides he wants to prosper in his soul, he is on the way to becoming spiritually minded. And becoming spiritually minded should be every Christian's goal.

Remember, Paul said, **For to be carnally minded is death, but to be spiritually minded is life and peace** (Rom. 8:6). To be spiritually minded requires a goal for change and a disciplined vision to take control of your destiny.

Proverbs 29:18 says, **Where there is no revelation, the people cast off restraint.** In the *King James Version* this verse reads, **Where there is no vision, the people perish.** So without a goal and a purpose, we ignore our own restraints; we don't apply discipline to our lives, and we perish. This is what the Greek word translated *restraint* in this verse actually says.[1]

The suicidal person is one with no hope, no vision of a future, no reason to go on in life. Vision is the reason people get out of bed, the reason we read books like this one, the reason we go on. It may be a vision of raising the kids, building a company, starting a ministry or buying a house. That vision will give you a certain amount of impetus to grow and change.

But as I said, most people don't stay with the vision of renewing their minds. It takes restraint, and it is too often easier to just flow downstream. It seems most people get caught at some point in life with a "maintenance" vision. The house is paid for, the kids are raised and the business is operating. But instead of seeking the Lord to see what He has in mind for them at that point in their lives, they try only to *maintain*.

Thinking they will enjoy life for a while, a lot of people kick back into maintenance mode. The problem is, you can't *maintain* in life. If you aren't moving forward, you're moving backward. It's like swimming upstream; you must either push ahead and swim, or get swept downstream and float downriver, wherever the current leads. You can soon feel unwanted or unimportant, and you can get depressed without understanding why. It's simply from a lack of vision, as we just read.

Many people die in their second year of retirement because of lack of vision or purpose. The physical problems that may arise are merely symptoms of the debilitating effects of stagnation in life. Many die shortly after the death of a spouse because their vision for life was as a team. When part of the team dies, they think the vision is over.

God wants us to stay young and live long. That means we must keep a vibrant vision of growth and change all our lives. We must make it the passion of our lives to be all we can be in God. Abundant life invites us to go as far as we can go with God and fulfill all that we can fulfill of His will. Paul, for example, said he finished his course and was ready to go on and be with the Lord. And you can finish your course too.

Renewing the Mind Key Number 28:

There's More to Life Than Making a Living

The goal of making a living is not a motivating vision; it is a *maintaining* one that will soon have you floating downriver, as it were. So many live to get the bills paid, take a vacation or buy more stuff. But when they get the stuff, there is an empty feeling that says, "Is that all there is?" There is more to life than that vision. But if you have a burning passion for God's will to be done in your life every day, you will have that spark of life.

GIDEON'S MASTER KEY

Remember Gideon of the Old Testament? He was a young man who had *no* vision. He saw himself as weak, poor and unable to do anything about his circumstances. Then one day the angel of the Lord came to him while he was hiding in a winepress, threshing out wheat to make some bread. He was afraid that the Midianites would find him and take away what little wheat he had for his family. Gideon was not a man who was making plans for his future. His goals were immediate and carnal. He was just trying to make a living.

The angel of the Lord said to Gideon in Judges 6:12, **"The Lord is with you, you mighty man of valor!"**

Now, these words were totally contrary to Gideon's mind-set, feelings and lifestyle. He had never been mighty as a champion, a warrior or a leader. He had never been a man of valor, honor, esteem or influence. He was a scared little guy, trying to get through life. But God said, "You are a mighty man of valor!"

The next few chapters of the book of Judges goes on to tell how the Lord took Gideon through a series of events that helped him renew his mind according to God's Word and purpose for his life.

But initially, Gideon argued with God that he was not a mighty man. In his own eyes, he was a loser and a failure. But the Lord wouldn't allow him to hang on to his mediocre lifestyle. Finally, Gideon accepted what God said about him, rejected what he had believed about himself for so long and made the great exchange. But there were three areas that God led Gideon to change before he could fulfill his destiny:

1) His self-esteem

2) His vision for life

3) And his relationships with people.

Gideon had to renew how he thought about himself, how he thought about his future and with whom he was involved. After making these changes, he went on to defeat the Midianites, breaking their bondage over his nation and becoming one of the greatest judges of Israel.

Gideon had the potential for greatness in him all the time. It wasn't that God made him something he hadn't been before. Everything Gideon needed was on the inside of him. God simply led him to release the things that were holding him back so he could go on to fulfill his destiny.

RENEWING THE MIND KEY NUMBER 29:

YOU ARE A MIGHTY MAN OR WOMAN OF VALOR, AND IT'S TIME YOU FOUND THE REAL YOU!

Gideon learned what it meant to become spiritually minded. No longer did the idolatrous folly of his backslidden nation, the daily needs of his immediate life or the fear of the enemy control his life. The needs of God and the welfare of others started directing this ordinary man's life. This was Gideon's master key. And it can be yours. I want you to meditate on some things:

- You have what it takes to make spiritual living the goal of your life.

- You have inside you the potential to make a difference in your family, city and nation.

- You have greatness in you if you are born again by the Spirit of God.

But remember, the reason that many Christians drift and stagnate in life is that they have no spiritual goals and never decide to go further.

Paul said that all of us run in a race, but only one wins. And runners can't win unless they finish the race. (1 Cor. 9:24.)

So as we continue from this point on in our spiritual journey, I want to give you some practical lifestyle exercises that will help you stay on track with God. Believing that God has made available to you the ability to grow up into His image is the first step in the process of transformation. Growing up into His image through discipline from that point on is always up to you.

STEPS TO PERSONAL TRANSFORMATION

1. Do I feel motivated to fulfill my full potential?

   _____

   _____

2. What is my vision for the future? Do I have the drive to discipline myself for change in my life? Am I holding the master key?

   _____

   _____

3. What aspects of my life am I merely maintaining?

   _____

   _____

4. How could I relate my situation in life to Gideon's?

   _____

   _____

5. Have I decided to be the mighty person of valor that God has called me to be?

   _____

   _____

16

If you try to change your attitudes or behavior without dealing with your basic mind-set, the changes will only be temporary. So next I want us to look at how the mind works.

HOW THE MIND WORKS

Your mind is the control center of your entire life. So in essence, when you change your thinking, you change your whole life. That can happen in a negative or a positive way. It depends on the image you have of God, which will determine how you see yourself. When you change your thought processes in a positive way and see God for who He really is, you will begin to see positive changes in every aspect of your life. But if you see God as old, mean and nervous and make negative changes, you will see these kind of changes overtake you in every aspect of your life.

PROGRAMMING STARTS BEFORE BIRTH

Our image of God is developed as we grow and progress through life. But did you know that even before you were born, your mind was being "programmed"? Most people don't realize this, and many who do understand it don't use the concept on a day-to-day basis. You have existing programs in your mental "computer" that control the way you get out of bed, the way you handle your job and the way you respond to every activity each day of your life.

Most of the decisions you make aren't conscious decisions but are programmed, subconscious decisions.

Most of the fights you get into with your spouse aren't started by a conscious choice. The fights start through a subconscious choice, a programmed thought that causes us to respond to circumstances in a certain way.

So instead of recognizing what produced the conflict, we often say, "I don't like these events. I don't like this relationship. I don't like these circumstances. I don't like the way things are going." And we don't make changes because we don't realize that it first requires a subconscious change. The subconscious response must be "renovated," or renewed, to the point at which the memory banks have filed away programmed behavior.

The Bible calls this programmed behavior **the spirit of your mind** (Eph. 4:23). The apostle Paul wrote about the need for reprogramming, or renewing, to the church at Ephesus almost two thousand years ago:

> **Put off, concerning your former conduct, the old man which grows corrupt according to the deceitful lusts,** *and be renewed in the spirit of your mind,* **and that you put on the new man which was created according to God, in true righteousness and holiness.**
>
> **Ephesians 4:22-24**

In this passage, Paul told the people of that church that each of them must renew the spirit of his mind in order to put on the new man, who is righteous, holy and prosperous in every way.

As you renew the spirit of your mind, that programmed way of thinking begins to change. When you exchange your old thinking patterns for God's thinking patterns, you begin to see new opportunities in relationships, business, finances and everything you do.

Now, I believe those programmed thoughts were stored away in your subconscious mind even before you were born. It is a normal part of development to store information in "the spirit of the mind." As a child is developing in its mother's womb, it gathers data. Before the child is even born it has collected data about the world it will enter. It can ask, *Is my world peaceful, or is it troubled? Is my world happy, or is it sad? Is my world successful, or is it struggling?*

As the child moves through childhood, additional programs are fed into the memory banks. The primary sources of input are parents, grandparents, baby-sitters and so on. Their attitudes become the child's attitudes. Their lifestyle becomes the child's lifestyle. Even their gestures become the child's gestures. The spirit of their minds become part of the spirit of the child's mind. The child's soul is shaped by their images.

My wife Wendy and I have three small children, and we have seen them all reflect our images right before our eyes. Our attitudes, both positive and negative, became part of them even before they are consciously aware of it.

Now this direct imprinting may be positive if your parents were fulfilled, healthy, loving people. But it can be negative if your parents were unhappy, sick, unloving people. If those "programmers" struggled through life and gave you the concept that life is a struggle, it's likely your life will be miserable.

Over and over, it has been proven that as we grow up, we repeat the good and bad examples of our parents. As you know, the alcoholic parent very often produces alcoholic children. The abusive parent frequently produces abusive children and the depressed parent often produces depressed children.

The sins or the blessings of the parents are passed on to the third and the fourth generation. (Num. 14:18.) The good *and* the bad are passed on, the Bible says.

THE PROCESS CONTINUES

As we began school and started going to church, other assumptions, beliefs, attitudes and thoughts began to be fed into our minds. We adopted them without realizing what we were adopting. Friends and relatives both contributed to this process. As we moved through the later school years and finally entered "the real world," the environment we accepted had much to do with the programmed spirit of our minds.

If you grew up in the South, you may have different attitudes toward home life than if you grew up in the North. If you grew up in Europe, the spirit of your mind will be very different than if you were raised in South America or North America.

Consciously, the attitudes and thoughts we grew up with don't necessarily control our lives, but subconsciously, they do. They control our lives every day without any conscious awareness.

For the first fifteen to twenty years of our lives, we put together this package of information called the spirit of the mind. It becomes our way of believing and our way of thinking. Sometime between fifteen and twenty years old, we conclude the gathering of information process and launch out into society to tackle life. We may continue in our education, and we may continue to gather technical data and other forms of information. But the spirit of our mind, the attitudes of our life and the ways in which we generally approach life are usually established before we are twenty.

For the rest of our lives, we just live out that programming. We simply follow through with the things we learned subconsciously, and we don't change very much from that point on.

Of course, this pattern can be broken by people like you who sincerely desire change and want God's best in your lifestyle. You can renew your mind, and more importantly, you can renew the spirit of your mind.

I am thrilled at your desire, because as we have seen, not many people change after their teen years. This is not to say that many people don't get a new job, move to a new city, meet their spouses, buy a new house or change their appearance. There are many things people change as they go through life, but the spirit of the mind usually isn't one of them.

Now, let me ask you something. As you have been reading, has it occurred to you how many times you act without thinking? You do that because somewhere in the past you were programmed to respond to certain situations in a particular way. Even after you are born again, your mind will still respond to certain situations in certain ways.

TIME-RELEASED BELIEFS

Before discussing the mechanism of change, we need to look at one more type of programming that I call *time-released beliefs*. This is the programming you don't realize is there until a specific incident brings it to the surface.

For example, the older I get, the more I realize that my mind is filled with time-released beliefs. When I was younger, I didn't really know what I believed about marriage, parenthood or any other major adult issues. But when I got married and began to raise children, new ways of thinking began to pop out that I didn't even know were part of my programming.

I will never forget the day my son, Caleb, was born. He was born at home. My wife and I and a few of our friends were there for the delivery. A couple of friends helped my wife, and I delivered the baby. Another friend made a video tape of the birth. When we played that tape later, I saw myself bathing and dressing our new son. And when I heard myself talking to Caleb, Wendy and our friends, I was amazed, shocked really, to hear myself speaking like my father. I saw his gestures and heard his tone and attitude when I talked to the baby!

It was then that I realized there had been a time-released belief preprogrammed in the spirit of my mind. That particular situation caused those programmed behaviors to be released, and I heard and saw myself doing things I never realized I would do.

As Caleb began to grow, he progressively stopped being a cute little baby who did everything right and became a typical little boy who did some things wrong. And again at this stage, I saw attitudes in myself and heard myself say the same words my father and mother had said to me when I was a little boy. I realized that although I had never thought those things and had not consciously decided to do those things, a programmed response in me surfaced as I dealt with my little boy. And many times, I didn't like what came out.

Maybe you remember your parents' disciplining you in a certain way, and you made this vow: "When I grow up and have kids, I'll never treat them that way!" I did. And yet, when I became a parent, there I was, doing the same things, carrying on the family tradition, so to speak. I was going through the same routines my parents went through without consciously deciding to do them. The spirit of my mind—my attitudes, beliefs and my ways of thinking about raising children—was not being freely and objectively developed to fit the different personalities of my children. My actions reflected time-released programs stored in my memory banks years before.

Many people struggle with problems without realizing they're not dealing with conscious decisions of today. They have no idea that they're responding with a way of thinking that has been hidden for years. And psychology can't do a thing about it.

The answer to overcoming these programming problems is to renew the mind, to renew the way you think. You can go to psychologists or psychiatrists and spend a lot of money trying to find out what Mom or Dad did and why you continue to struggle. But that can't teach you how to renew the spirit of your mind. You can go through hours and hours of therapy and still not see any change. Going back through the feelings, emotions and circumstances of the past may not change a thing. You may not progress at all. You may discover why you have your problems, but you'll still have the problems. You may know why you think the way you think, but you will still think the way you think!

What I have been showing you is how to *change* those things that are keeping you from the best God has to offer. Mind renewal can keep those old attitudes and beliefs from stopping the process of change.

As a parent I saw myself acting the same way my own parents had acted. I also began to realize that the way I made financial decisions was also a programmed response I learned from my parents. Now remember, I was born again when I was married. And even then, I learned that my decisions weren't based on what would most likely bring financial success. They were based on attitudes toward money, possessions and spending I had adopted as I was growing up. So I often found myself struggling financially because of the foolish things I did. I didn't want to struggle constantly, but I continued to do foolish things until I renewed my mind about finances.

I see people every day in the same situation who are fed up with the way they are living. They don't like the way things are going. But they don't change, because they haven't found the key to change.

Now, let me make this clear: Not *everything* you do is patterned after what you saw growing up. Sometimes when we make a vow not to do what our parents did, we react *against* the things we saw and do act the opposite way. In this case, some things you do today are exactly the opposite of what your parents did. However, your attitudes, beliefs and behavior are *still programmed responses*. The spirit of your mind is simply programmed to respond in a way that is opposite to your parents' behavior. But your life today is still being controlled by the past, although it is a reactionary control.

Learning Is Not Changing

Another thing you must understand is that *learning is not changing*. Acquiring knowledge doesn't automatically renew your mind. More knowledge of the psychological and sociological circumstances of your past or present won't necessarily change your life.

Well-educated people are among those whose lives are total failures. Living in a land of opportunity, many people still suffer and struggle. Some even end their lives in suicide. Many people with a good education suffer from drug and alcohol abuse. So learning can be an asset—and I'm all for it—but education isn't the key to *real* change in your life. What we have been talking about is *mind renewal,* as the Bible calls it.

The will of God is for you to live a prosperous, successful life. Spiritually, mentally, physically, financially and socially, God desires the fullness of His abundant life and prosperity for you. It is never His will for people to suffer or struggle through life. Suffering and struggling come when we are living contrary to His will for us.

You may think it's hard to live according to the will of God, but the Bible says it is hard to live the way of the transgressor. (Prov. 13:15 KJV.) Living in the will of God is the highest kind of life any man or woman will ever experience.

How do we get there? By the transformation of our minds! And the Holy Spirit will help us do it, as we give ourselves totally to Him.

A Caterpillar Is a Butterfly in Disguise

Let's review the word *transformed* from Romans 12:2. Literally, it means "metamorphosis," or "a complete change in form." If the people in the Roman church were willing to be changed, Paul wrote to them, they could have the highest kind of life. And if that was true for them, it is still true for us today.

A caterpillar may look up at a butterfly flying through the air and say, "Man, he's got it made in the shade! Here I am down here, living on this twig and barely crawling along. My whole world is wrapped up in this little branch. I have to eat these funny little leaves, and the best I can do is get a new branch with new leaves. But that guy is flying!"

He watches the butterfly flutter overhead, bright, colorful and free, flying everywhere and experiencing a very exciting life. But the caterpillar can also have this same life if he is willing to go through a metamorphosis. You know how the process works: The caterpillar spins a cocoon, puts himself into an uncomfortable position for a while, and then through the process of time, he is changed completely. He becomes totally different. He is transformed and leaves his cocoon as a butterfly.

Isn't that an exciting process! I hope you view the process of change that way by now. When you think of spreading your wings, having a whole new outlook on life, entering into a whole new realm, it should be exciting! But to get there, you must go through a metamorphosis.

The metamorphosis of mind renewal means to change or exchange. For example, if someone who was working for me continued to be unproductive in spite of the fact that I did everything I could to bring change into his life, I might have to *exchange* him for someone else. I might have to "put off" that old worker to "put on someone new" in that position to get the job done the way it should be done. (Remember Ephesians 4:22-24.)

In the same way, if your way of thinking hasn't brought the results you want—after you tried learning more, reading more, attending more improvement seminars or even getting another job—then you must *make an exchange* in your mind, the control center of your life.

The **good and acceptable and perfect will of God** Romans 12:2 talks about makes the highest kind of spiritual, mental, physical, financial and social success.

When does that come? When you are transformed.

How do you get transformed? By renewing your mind.

Your mind is renewed by taking out the old thoughts and old attitudes, removing the old spirit of the mind and gaining a new way of thinking. When this happens, the spirit of your mind is transformed and you enter into a new life.

WHY PEOPLE RESIST CHANGE

Many people resist change because they have tried to change but have failed, and they don't want to fail again. How many times have you tried to change? By now you know that wanting to change isn't enough; you must be completely *transformed*. A mental *exchange* needs to take place. You must remove some things from your thinking and replace them with new programming. If you know how, change is not all that difficult.

If you have been resisting change because you think people around you are controlling you or trying to change you, then you *really* need to renew your mind. *You have really missed it.* You are millions of miles from the source of your problem. You have your finger pointed at everyone else, instead of yourself. You have put the blame on other people, who really have no control over your thinking, and have neglected the one who does control you—you!

Your life is not at the mercy of everyone else. Yes, other people can affect you, and they can have a certain amount of influence over you. But you decide how that influence will affect you. You decide if a mountain is a platform to blast off from to reach great heights or a hindrance that will stop you in your tracks.

You decide if difficulties will make you stronger so you can overcome problems easily or if they will defeat you and keep you from moving ahead. Every time you allow God's Word into the spirit of your mind through meditation, an exchange takes place. But you are always in control of the renewing process. You are the only one who can really make your life what you want it to be. It's God's will for everyone, but you must participate in the process.

I also know that as long as you point the finger at others, you will never change, you will never grow and your life will be stagnant until you die.

Remember, to renew or to exchange your mind is a lot like changing a baby's diaper. As a father of young children, I can relate to this image because, believe me, I have changed many diapers!

When your children need their diapers changed, they begin to fuss because they are uncomfortable. Then they begin to smell, and the odor makes everyone else uncomfortable! So what do you do? A wise parent grabs the baby, sprinkles a little powder on him and puts on a clean diaper.

But wait a minute! I left out that important step we looked at earlier—you must take off the dirty diaper first.

Many of us are going through life with stinking thinking, and we need a diaper change *really bad*. Our "diapers"—the state of our minds—cause our whole lives to stink. We need changing, but sometimes all we do is sprinkle a little powder on top of the old diaper and try to clean ourselves up by putting a clean diaper over the old one. And this doesn't solve the problem. Very soon, the "odor" can be detected again. To eliminate the problem and exchange a dirty diaper for a clean one, there is a proper procedure to follow.

First, as it is with babies, you remove the old diaper and clean up the baby. Then when the baby is clean and fresh, you put on the new diaper. When that process of change takes place the baby is comfortable and no longer makes others uncomfortable.

The same is true of renewing the mind and the spirit of the mind. If you don't remove old programmed thoughts but merely try to add new thoughts on to your old way of thinking, you aren't going to change very much. This is why many people never make lasting changes in their lives. They just continue adding on to the same old way of thinking instead of changing it once and for all.

Look at what frequently happens with divorce and remarriage. Nine times out of ten, the second marriage is no better than the first. The only difference is the name of the spouse you fight with. Why? Because when you marry the second time, *you* bring the same *you* into that marriage you brought into the first one.

What happens when you change jobs because you had problems with the last one? Usually, there is not much improvement. You might make a little more money and even be able to buy a nicer car or house. But the same you who was part of the problem at the first job is the same you operating in the second job. Eventually, you may feel the same way about your new job. You may go through the same kind of problems, struggle with the same difficulties and basically continue in the same direction.

So changing outward circumstances doesn't always affect your life very much. Adding to your knowledge or possessions doesn't change your life in any real way. What works is taking off the old and replacing it with the new.

Remember, when you change the inside, the outside will take care of itself. When you plant the proper seed in your mind, you are going to find the fruit that you are looking for.

Jesus said:

> **"A good man out of the good treasure of his heart brings forth good things; and an evil man out of the evil treasure brings forth evil things."**

Matthew 12:35

Look at what Jesus is saying in this verse. Out of your heart, you will bring forth good things or evil things.

What determines what you bring forth? Heredity, good luck or the environment in which you live? No, what determines what comes out of you is simply *what is already in you.* Your life is a manifestation of what is in you. Your marriage is a manifestation of what is in you concerning marriage. Your children are a manifestation of what is in you concerning children. Your finances are a manifestation of what is in you concerning finances. Your business or job is a manifestation of what is in you concerning work.

It is the "treasure" that is inside you that produces change, not additional learning or exterior changes. And when you change the treasure, you will change what is brought forth.

I want to finish this chapter with two illustrations. First, I'm sure you have heard of the apartment projects the government often builds to get people out of the slums. But have you heard what often happens within a year? The beautiful new housing development is run-down, filthy and in the same poverty-stricken condition the people there came from. Why? Because the programmed thinking the people had about their living condition wasn't exchanged for new thinking. They thought and acted like slum tenants even in new housing, so their new housing took on the look of their internal image.

The external is always a manifestation of the internal. If we try to impose external changes, our internal programmed thinking will cause us to do whatever is necessary to bring things "back to normal." People will fit whatever subconscious program is directing them in life to their living situation. They will lose it, destroy it, blow it or whatever else is necessary to get back to their concept of normal.

The second illustration has to do with a study that was done in Canada on a group of a hundred lottery winners. These were people who had won over a million dollars cash. The study took place over a period of more than twenty years and showed that over 90 percent of those lottery winners had nothing to show for their winnings after about twenty years. Why? They thought poor, so they ended up poor. They blew their millions and returned to the "normal" existence they'd had before they had won the lottery.

So it is only when you change internally that you see a sustained change externally. If you don't change inside, no matter what happens, sooner or later, you will get back to what is "normal" for you.

Take some time to reflect on the thought processes that have been programmed into your mind. How they got there and what you can do about it is part of the renewal process. You can't just put a clean diaper over old stinking thinking. Remember, you may be walking and talking the Christian walk, but eventually those old stinking thoughts will try to reclaim you. You don't have to allow it!

It takes courage to discover those areas of programmed responses that may still be holding you back. But it will be worth the time and effort to get God's good treasure built up in your mind. Consider this chapter's personal application keys carefully. Take your time before moving to the next chapter. Write your thoughts down, and ask God to give you insight into how to change.

KEYS TO PERSONAL APPLICATION

"Your mind is the control center of your life."

1. How have your family/parent relationships affected the spirit of your mind and current relationships? Think about your current attitudes and thought processes that haven't changed since you came to the Cross.

   _____

   _____

2. In what specific areas of your life do you desire change?

   _____

   _____

3. What beliefs and/or behavior didn't come up in your life until you started this study?

_____

_____

4. In what areas of your life have you resisted change?

_____

_____

17

WHAT IS YOUR
MENTAL NET WORTH?

There is an accounting process in the financial world that reveals what your monetary assets and liabilities are. The assets and liabilities are added together to show whether you are in a positive or negative situation. The bottom line is the net worth.

In this chapter, I want you to take stock of your mental inventory and find the balance between your mental assets and liabilities. If the assets outweigh the liabilities, you are experiencing a happy and productive life. If not, you are probably experiencing many problem areas in your life.

It is time to know at this stage of our study what has been fed into your memory bank. If it is good treasure, it will bring you great returns. If it isn't good treasure, then what you are storing up will bring destruction. (Matt. 12:35.)

I also want to give you five practical steps to ensure that you are building a positive future in Christ.

WHEN YOUR MIND CHANGES, YOUR LIFE CHANGES

Renewing your mind involves changes in your conscious thinking. But even more important in the renewal process are the changes that take place in the spirit of your mind.

Important changes in your life are manifestations of the inward changes you have made. So we need to focus on the inward things. People are so often concerned with changing outward things that all their time is spent dealing with them, and they never get to the true root of change. Consequently, in spite of all the time they spend trying to change, very few things ever really change.

In the last chapter, we saw that our minds are the controlling mechanisms of our lives—computers that store information and control the way things happen. Your mind controls decisions and choices. In your family, business, finances, health and all you do, your mind is the controlling mechanism. So to the degree that your mind is renewed is the degree of change and a renewed life that you will experience.

If you continue to focus on the outward things, you will miss the changes that are possible. The aches, sniffles and fever that go with a cold, for example, aren't the cold, but they are the symptoms of it. They aren't the problem but manifestations of the problem. And dealing with the symptoms of a cold does cure you of the same cold.

In the same way, most of us only deal with life's symptoms. We focus on outward things and look at circumstances. Because we spend our time focused on the symptoms, we don't get to the root cause of the problem.

Whatever is stored in you is either good or bad treasure, and that is what you bring forth every day. Perhaps your stored treasure is partly good and partly bad. You may not have "evil" treasure inside you, but you may have mediocre treasure.

I believe Christians today are tired of mediocrity. But being tired of it doesn't mean you know how to change it. Being tired of where you are is simply an expression of your frustration. And weary frustration won't produce any changes.

When you begin to change the spirit of your mind, you quit dealing with the outward symptoms of failure in life and begin to change the kind of treasure that is within you. Your mind isn't the totality of that treasure; it is only one part of it. However, it *is* a major part and the key to changing all of the treasure.

Jesus said, **"For where your treasure is, there your heart will be also"** (Matt. 6:21). So Jesus said your heart contains the treasure, and your heart is the place where your soul and spirit meet. Your "treasure" is made up of thoughts, beliefs, assumptions and doctrines that you accept as true. Your treasure is what you base your decisions and attitudes on; it can bring success, or it can bring failure.

In other words, your treasure is what you live on. All you do every day of your life comes out of that treasure. It is a "bank account" for life. You draw on that bank account and withdraw "currency" to deal with your spouse. You make a withdrawal every time you are with friends and neighbors. You make a withdrawal when you interact with other people on your job or at your business.

Every day, all of us make withdrawals from the treasure in our hearts. If your treasure is negative, a withdrawal may bring the currency of worry, strife or contention.

If things around you are negative, that is a reflection of what you've stored away in your heart. If you're struggling financially, your treasure, so to speak, may be a poverty mentality. If you're continually experiencing sickness and disease, your treasure may be a sickness mentality. You see, your physical condition will produce the outward symptoms of the treasure that is in your heart. And every day you bring that treasure forth, you will experience its outward problems.

Your Treasure Is Reflected as Symptoms

If you've been divorced or are having problems in your marriage, you or your spouse may have "treasure" stored up that is contrary to a successful marriage.

It's easy to spot the things in your treasure that need changing by looking at the negative symptoms you see in your life. It's also easy to spot your good treasure from the successful, fruitful manifestations that show up in your life every day.

You can see what is inside you by what is coming out of you. Every problem in your life is like a printed page from your mind, held up for all to read. We *live out* our thinking. The importance of understanding this isn't so you can figure out what is wrong with everyone else but so you can look at yourself and see where you need to improve.

This valuable truth is a puzzle to many people, but the Holy Spirit gave it to us very plainly in Scripture:

> Then He called the multitude and said to them, "Hear and understand: Not what goes into the mouth defiles a man; but what comes out of the mouth, this defiles a man."
>
> Then His disciples came and said to Him, "Do You know that the Pharisees were offended when they heard this saying?"
>
> But He answered and said, "Every plant which My heavenly Father has not planted will be uprooted. Let them alone. They are blind leaders of the blind. And if the blind leads the blind, both will fall into a ditch."
>
> Then Peter answered and said to Him, "Explain this parable to us."
>
> So Jesus said, "Are you also still without understanding? Do you not yet understand that whatever enters the mouth goes into the stomach and is eliminated? But those things which proceed out of the mouth come from the heart, and they defile a man."
>
> Matthew 15:10-18

In the verse following this passage, verse 19, Jesus went on to list the kinds of things that come from the heart:

> "For out of the heart proceed evil thoughts, murders, adulteries, fornications, thefts, false witness, blasphemies."

In verse 20 Jesus says the things He listed are those that defile you, not the outward things:

"These are the things which defile a man, but to eat with unwashed hands does not defile a man."

In these passages particularly Jesus teaches us how the thoughts of our minds translate into outward behavior and lifestyle.

A homosexual person may say, "I was born this way. This is natural for me" No, God made man, and God made woman; He didn't make a man in a woman's body or a woman in a man's body. God doesn't make mistakes. God made Adam and Eve, not Adam and Steve.

A person is a homosexual because he or she began to think, *Maybe I'm that way. I need to explore all the possibilities.* The first little thought was a seed that multiplied into a great negative harvest. The seed might also have been an emotional problem relating to the opposite sex brought about by a bad relationship with a mother or father. Those thoughts and emotions then produce a negative, destructive homosexual lifestyle.

Every Action Begins With a Thought

Jesus said that even murder begins with a thought. So where do financial dilemmas come from? Where do emotional dilemmas come from? They come from the thoughts of the heart.

What I have been striving to show you is that you can *change* the treasure of your heart. Once you change that treasure, you can begin to make positive withdrawals. You can bring forth new things that will end your problems.

When your mind is renewed, you can bring forth love and peace. You can bring forth forgiveness and patience and all of the other positive things of life. But when your mind is negative, you bring forth disagreement, strife and bitterness. You bring forth anger and depression.

But remember, those negative things don't just fall on you! Bitterness, anger and depression don't come on you from the outside.

They aren't little clouds that float around the country and every once in a while sprinkle their rain on you.

People use the old saying, "I got up on the wrong side of the bed," to excuse the bad things that come out of the negative treasure of their hearts. The side of the bed you get up on has nothing to do with the fruit in your life. It's the thoughts you get up with and take into your day that produce the negative results.

Others may say, "Well, I'm just in a bad mood." No, it isn't a "mood"; it is a way of thinking. Someone else would say, "I must be under a dark cloud today." And that's also just a way of rationalizing negative thinking.

When your way of thinking changes, how you live changes. You *choose* what goes on in your life. You choose how far you will go.

Life is a choice. This principle is described quite strongly in Deuteronomy 30:19:

> **"I call heaven and earth as witnesses today against you, that I have set before you life and death, blessing and cursing; therefore choose life, that both you and your descendants may live."**

These words of God spoken to the ancient people of Israel are just as vital to us today. Life and death, blessings or cursings, are set before us to choose. Which do you want? Which will you choose? The choice isn't up to your family, the government or your company. It isn't even up to your spouse. *You* choose life or death.

The choices you've made up to this point have built your inward treasure, and what you are experiencing in your life is the consequence of what you think and believe. You control what you choose. But after you make that choice, it controls you. So choose carefully!

CYCLES OF LIFE

When I counsel couples having marital problems, sometimes one of them will say, "I really believe that if I would leave my spouse, my life would be a lot better." So I talk with the couple about how they can improve their marriage and how they can resolve their differences and problems. But when they come back a week later, the one will say, "Well, I tried to do what you said, but I'm still thinking about divorce. If I could get away, it would be different and everything would be better."

When I ask people in this situation how often they've tried to solve things by leaving, too often they answer, "This is my second marriage," "This is my third," or "I've left several times and come back."

In other words, they have created a way of thinking that says, "If I could only get out of this marriage and find someone new, something different, my life would be better."

I tell these kinds of people that their current marriage is no better than their previous one. They are still the same people. Their problem has nothing to do with their spouse. They are the problem. But they continue holding on to the belief that if they change spouses they would have a better life—even though changing spouses the last time didn't make life better.

When you accept the thought that outward things must change before you can feel differently, you are locked into a never-ending cycle. You have become a lifetime "runner." You run from relationships, from responsibilities and from change. And you will end up running from the very thing that can make a difference in your life—the renewing of your mind. But if you will stop running, break the habit of rebelling against God's way of changing and choose a new way of thinking, your life will change.

A wise person once said, "Everywhere you go, there you are." That may sound simple, but it really is profound. You may try to run, but you have to take yourself along wherever you go. If you have wrong thoughts, it creates bad situations. You may try to find escape by running from yourself, but the thing that made the initial situation bad—your mind—will come with you into the next situation.

By renewing the spirit of your mind, you can break this cycle. With God's help, you can stretch yourself to change your thinking so your mental net worth will increase and your problems won't be repeated over and over again. So start now taking stock of your mental net worth in order to improve the quality of the treasure that is flowing out of your heart.

THE 5 RS OF CHANGE

As I said, I like action steps. You know—individual lifestyle directives that break down a truth into simple operations. So I want to give you five steps that will not only assist you in assessing your current mental net worth but will help you bring change to every realm of your life. These steps will work in marriage, finances, physical health and raising children. If you make it a point to act on them, they can bring lasting change. I call them the five Rs, and they will work for you.

R STEP 1: *RESPONSIBILITY*

TAKE RESPONSIBILITY FOR YOURSELF AND YOUR LIFE

The first R of realizing your mental net worth and changing it is to take *responsibility*. Take full responsibility for yourself and your life. Don't blame God for the condition of your life. Don't blame your spouse. And don't blame your neighbor or your boss. Take full responsibility. If you don't, nothing else will help you. If you don't accept complete responsibility for the condition of your life, nothing will work. Until you take full responsibility, you will remain out of control, incapable of change. You will be sentenced to a life of maintenance, running like mad just to stay in the same place. *So take full responsibility for yourself.*

R STEP 2: *RETHINK*

RETHINK WHAT YOU BELIEVE

The second R of change is to *rethink*. Rethink what you believe and what you assume is true. Rethink what you believe is right and what you assume is the way to handle life. Rethink those concepts for living which you developed growing up. If you don't begin to rethink some of your concepts, you will continue to live and make decisions based on thinking that is totally wrong. *So rethink what you think.*

R STEP 3: *REJECT*

REJECT YOUR OLD WAYS

The third R of change is to *reject*. Reject your old ways. Reject the old thoughts that come back to you and block your ability to change. This is one of the most difficult steps, because the old habits of thinking are hard to break. Many times, when I said I was going to change and think a new way, I found myself slipping back into the old way again.

Let me give you a practical example. My wife Wendy and I have discussed a behavior of mine many times. She will say to me, "You don't talk to me enough about your feelings and share your thoughts with me. You pick up a magazine or turn on the television instead of talking to me, and that makes me feel unimportant!"

So I say to myself, *I'm going to change this pattern and begin to communicate and share with my wife. I'm not going to pick up a magazine or a book. I'll just relax and share with her.*

I *really* want to do it. I know this is the right decision. I think about it and decide to start a new way of thinking. Then the next thing I know, I'm right back where I started. I go through the same old habits and patterns, my wife is frustrated again and I hear her say the same thing again: "You always do that! You always pick up a magazine, or you turn on the television. Why don't you change?"

I *want* to change, and I have decided to change—but before I know it, here I am, doing the same thing again. I know you can relate to this kind of pattern when it comes to losing weight, managing money or communicating with your spouse. There are many behavior patterns we all have in common.

What I have to do is reject my old way of thinking every time it comes back. When the thought comes to me to pick up a magazine or do something by myself, I must reject it *before* I follow through with the action. I have to bring it captive to the Word. And this is an important part of the mind renewal process.

To break that habit of acting without thinking, I must be alert to catch that triggering thought and push it out of my mind. I must consciously take hold of that thought and say, *No! This is a negative thought. I don't want to do this, and I'm not going to do it.* This stops the cycle before it becomes action.

Letting negative thoughts become actions and repenting with continual resolutions to do better in the future simply won't break the negative cycle. The way to break it is to catch it when it starts to run and stop it. After a few times, the cycle will be broken. But you must reject the cycle right on the spot, right then while it is trying to repeat itself. Don't go through the old routine again. *Reject that old way of thinking.*

R STEP 4: *REVIEW*

REVIEW YOUR NEW WAY OF THINKING

The fourth R of change is to *review*. Review, or practice, your new way of thinking. Meditate on the Word. Practice thinking these new thoughts. When you're driving your car, instead of "spacing out" listening to some ungodly, depressed radio personality, practice your new way of thinking. Instead of wasting your mental time, take the time to think.

In the example I gave you about changing the way I communicate with my wife, I began to practice a new way of thinking when I was driving, when I was eating lunch and when I was in my office alone. I would practice these thoughts: *I just love to talk with Wendy. I enjoy communicating and sharing with her. It's good to have a lovely wife with whom I can sit and talk and share myself and tell her how I think and feel. I really enjoy it.*

Now, in the past I didn't enjoy it because I was turned inward and locked into the habit of staying quiet. But when I began to renew my way of thinking, I learned to enjoy communicating with my wife.

You have to review and practice a new way of thinking, or it will never become a part of you. Go over it and over it and over it. You can call it meditation, or you can call it practicing. But it really is reviewing your new thoughts.

Suppose you have a problem with money. Perhaps you consistently spend all of your money before you earn it. Your credit cards are charged to the limit, so you get another one and charge it to the limit too! Perhaps you're barely getting by and are behind in your payments. You really need to practice a new way of thinking. You need to review new thoughts about handling money. Instead of watching television, begin reviewing a new way of thinking.

Think, *I enjoy living debt free. It feels good to pay for things when I buy them, not six months or a year later. It's nice to have money in the bank and have all my bills paid. I'm disciplined with my money. I only spend money I have after I've paid my bills and have saved some money to invest in my future. I am in control of my finances!*

Now, as you review these new thoughts, you are practicing a new way to think about money. So when you get into a store and see something you really can't afford, your new way of thinking will allow you to say to yourself, *Nah, I'm not going to buy that because I'm a good money manager. I'm disciplined in my spending. I invest my money. I save my money. I don't blow my money.*

By reviewing these new thoughts, you strengthen your new lifestyle and bring change into your life.

R Step 5: *Resound*

Let Your Thoughts Resound Out Loud

The fifth R of change is to *resound*. This means to speak your new thoughts so they "resound" out loud. Just like reviewing, which is thinking to yourself, you also have to speak your thoughts out loud. I've found that if you don't speak out your new way of thinking, it will never become a new way of thinking, which means you will never change anything in your life. You have to speak your new thoughts out loud.

Perhaps your wife has confronted you about spending more time together as a family, and you respond with, "Well, I bring home money for you. Isn't that good enough?"

No, it isn't! Your wife wants *you* more than she wants money. In order to change, you must allow the new thoughts to resound from your mouth.

You might start saying things like, "I love spending time with my wife and family. I love communicating and sharing with my family. I love to go home and spend evenings with my family."

If your problem is money, maybe you've been saying, "Every time I get any money, it just seems to slip through my fingers. It just disappears. I don't know where all the money goes. I can't hang on to money; I must have holes in my pocket. Someone must be stealing from my bank account. I've never been able to save money."

As long as you speak out the problem and repeat what is wrong, you will continue doing more of what is wrong. But when you begin to say something new and start saying the way you want your life to be, you will have what you say.

So the last R of mind renewal in this chapter is letting the new thoughts in your mind resound by speaking your new way of thinking.

FIVE RS SUMMARY

It is important for you to have a solid grip on these five Rs of effective change, so I will review them quickly.

Number one is to be *responsible*. Many people avoid taking responsibility to the point that they have no control over their situations. Without control, you can't change anything. But the truth is, you *are* in control. And the responsibility to change is yours.

Number two is to *rethink*. Challenge what you believe, what you assume to be true and what you've been told. When an unbiblical belief system and inborn thoughts and actions surface, challenge and rethink them. This will give your new thoughts a chance to prove themselves.

Number three is to *reject* the old way. If your old thoughts have produced the problems you have today, make room for their replacement by rejecting your old thoughts.

Number four is to *review* the new. You need to capture new thoughts, but going over them once isn't enough. In order to have them work, you need to imprint them deeply in your mind by reviewing and practicing your new thinking over and over again.

Number five is to let your new thoughts *resound*. This means to speak them. Repeat new thoughts to yourself, and speak them to your family and friends. This is the secret ingredient that will create permanent change in you. Speaking thoughts out loud will lock them permanently in your mind, and positive results will surely follow.

If you act on these five Rs—responsibility, rethinking, rejecting, reviewing and resounding—you will start the process of change. You will bring new things into your life. You will change the treasure in your heart. Then you will have something new to draw from that will make a difference in your life.

Many people are "waiting for their ship to come in." Even if their ship does come in, their thinking would sink it in the harbor! So remember, it isn't a matter of waiting for something to happen outside of you; it is a matter of changing something inside of you.

Remember 3 John 2 KJV: **You will prosper and be in health, even as thy soul prospereth.**

A prosperous soul is what I hope this book is helping you possess. A prosperous soul has an abundance of peace, joy and prosperity in every realm of life. These things must be in you before they can be *around* you. They have to come out of your heart. A prosperous soul is the beginning of a prosperous life.

Living in a prosperous country doesn't guarantee that you will be prosperous. We see people in the richest country in the world living on the streets without a place to sleep. They live on sidewalks and sleep in parks, or they live in run-down, filthy places. Yet they live in a nation with more opportunities to prosper than you can imagine.

I recently saw a man holding a big sign that said, "No job, no food, no money. Please help!" He had a bucket in front of him, and he wanted people to put money in it. As I drove past him, I thought, *Boy, that is sad. What a tragedy. I feel for that man.* There he was, waving his sign at all the cars going past. Yet within a mile, I passed four businesses with "Help Wanted" signs. Four of them! Instead of standing there waiting for someone to come and change his circumstances for him, he could have changed his own circumstances.

Now this doesn't mean I don't have compassion for him or other disadvantaged people. But the fact remains that if we took all the money in the world and dispersed it evenly to every person, there is enough wealth in our world for everyone to have approximately $12 million dollars. This includes everyone in China, India and Africa and every man, woman and child on earth.

But if we disposed of all the wealth today, within five years, all of it would be back in the same hands again, and most of those who are poor today would be poor again.

The point is, it is our mental net worth that controls what comes out of us. Our thoughts, the treasure of our heart—whether they be good or bad beliefs and attitudes—are what control our lives.

There is no fountain of youth. There is no get-rich-quick scheme. No one is going to change everything around you and make your life better. You can prosper outwardly when you begin to prosper inwardly. By renewing the spirit of your mind, you can begin to change your life.

Out of the good treasure of your heart, you will bring forth a good life. Out of the negative treasure of your heart, you will continue to bring forth a negative life.

I want to ask you to take a good honest look at your circumstances to see whether the liabilities of your negative thoughts outweigh the assets of your good thoughts. If your heart is "running in the red," begin to make entries on the positive side. Then eliminate entries on the negative side until you have a positive balance.

Practice doing this often. And continually review the five Rs, because the quality of your heart's treasure is the key to your soul's prospering.

KEYS TO PERSONAL APPLICATION

"Your inner strengths and weaknesses are being
seen in your behavior and actions every day."

1. Write on a piece of paper "Assets" on one side and "Liabilities" on the other. If you are a giver and encouraging to others, write those qualities down under "Assets." If you are critical and struggle with

selfishness, write those negative qualities under "Liabilities." Keep this list as food for thought.

2. Do you believe your choices have brought you to where you are in life today?

_____

_____

3. Of the five Rs of change, which transformational step will be the most difficult for you?

_____

_____

18

FINDING YOUR
MENTAL "ROOTS"

Have you ever told anyone, "I've already made up my mind"? I think all of us have made statements like this to demonstrate that we're capable of making independent decisions. However, our "independent" decision is often made based on old information programmed into our minds. We simply retrieve old information from our subconscious minds and deliver it in the form of a "decision."

What happens if you have false information stored away? You will use it to make wrong decisions, and you won't even be aware of the stored information your mind used to make the following decision. So you need to learn how to discover those areas of your thinking that lead to bad decisions.

It's not difficult to change thought patterns, but it may not happen immediately. Changing your thinking does take time, and it requires using every one of the processes we have covered so far.

You can change *any* part of your life: physical, mental, spiritual, financial and social. *The key is changing your mind and your way of thinking.* You decide what you will think, and then your thinking determines what will happen in your life. So choose your thoughts carefully!

THE KEY TO CHANGE

Now I want to explore the area of the subconscious. The subconscious mind is discussed quite a bit by psychologists and psychiatrists, who work with behavioral change. They deal with some truth; but psychology is the world's interpretation of the mind. God's "psychology" is revealed in Scriptures, particularly ones that show the relationship of man's soul, body and spirit.

Your subconscious mind must be changed in order for your life to change. As we have seen, ways of thinking that you learned while growing up are still affecting many decisions in your life. The exciting thing is that you can change what has been stored in your subconscious, which in turn will change the choices and decisions you make.

Many of your decisions about marriage were programmed when you were a teenager. Many of your decisions about friendship and relationships were programmed years ago by things you experienced or learned in some other way.

By the time you reached your early teen years, your decisions about marriage, handling money and working were already formed. And now you are living out that programmed way of thinking.

I've worked with many people in prisons. If you talk to the average prisoner in a state penitentiary, county jail or city jail, you won't find many inmates who enjoy living behind bars. It is extremely rare to find someone who is happier locked up than free. A majority of prisoners want to get out, yet most of them who do get out of prison will end up back again.

You may say, "If they don't like prison, why do they live the kinds of lives that will ensure their return?"

The reason is that their subconscious minds are programmed with antisocial thinking, so they automatically move back into that kind of life. Eventually they get caught again and are returned to prison. They will tell you, "I don't like living like this; it's terrible." Yet most of them will never change. They will continue to approach life the same way and have the same problems year after year after year.

And that doesn't just happen with prisoners. I have seen this same kind of thinking with ordinary people on a daily basis. Certain individuals or families have continual financial problems. They barely get by and barely make ends meet. Even if they got a $500-a-month raise in income, within the month that money would also be spent and they would be in the same situation.

Most people believe that if they had more money, they would live better and be better off. Yet when they do make more, they often get into more financial bondage and have more debt to struggle with. This is not to say that you shouldn't make more money. I believe you should. But the key to prosperity isn't a better salary; the key to prosperity is to renew your mind so that when you do make more money, you will be able to manage it properly.

What do you really want out of life? Do you find yourself moving farther and farther away from what you want in spite of everything you do? Is there some hidden programmed thinking preventing you from success and fulfillment? Then let's take a look into your thinking process and find out how to make it produce what you really want.

Reflex Thinking

I want to share some keys that will enable you to change the spirit of your mind's subconscious processes so you can make choices that line up with the Word of God. I want you to avoid going through the same difficulties over and over again.

First, I want you to think about the term *reflex thoughts*. There are muscles in the human body that were created to react to stimuli without any conscious thought. Your lungs are reflex *organs*, or automatic reaction systems. You don't have to think about breathing or tell yourself to breathe. Your heart is also a reflex organ. As you read this book, you aren't thinking about keeping your heart going, because the heart does its work automatically.

If you hit your leg right below the kneecap, you will see a muscle react automatically—your leg will jump without your telling it to. As a matter of fact, it will still react even if you try to stop it!

You also have thoughts that operate just like that. All the thoughts in your subconscious are reflex thoughts. Those thoughts are the ones that automatically trigger certain words, behaviors and patterns in your life. They are thoughts you aren't thinking for the first time.

Unfortunately, most of our lives are spent reacting to the reflex thoughts in our subconscious. We may think we're in charge of our lives, but in reality we're not; our subconscious is—if we allow it. We think we're making independent decisions, but in reality, we're making reflex decisions.

Just as there are physical habits that must be broken, there are thinking habits that must also be broken. In today's world, for example, no one thinks smoking tobacco is beneficial. And I doubt if there are any people who still think smoking is harmless! Yet many people still smoke. The health hazards of smoking, the expense and the unpleasantness of the smoke have been part of smoking since tobacco was first imported.

However, it took a national campaign linking smoking with an increased risk of cancer to cause many people to change the program in their subconscious mind that said, *Smoking is harmless. Smoking is actually pleasant. I have to smoke, and no one is going to make me quit if I don't want to!*

Even after changing the thought programming, many people haven't been able to change this particular reflex because of the fight against the physical addiction.

Most smokers don't think about lighting the first cigarette they smoke in the morning. They just get up, automatically grab a cigarette and light it without ever making a conscious decision to do so. That is called a habit. They never think about getting a cigarette out of the pack, lighting the match, sucking the smoke into their lungs and blowing out the match. Those things have become reflex actions.

There are so many examples like this in our everyday lives: drinking coffee, driving to and from work, washing the dishes and so forth. After a few times of doing something the same way, we tend to file that thing away as a *program*. And from then on, we do that particular thing without ever thinking about it.

How do we do this? Out of habit. These things become habits because of the subconscious part of our minds. When God created the subconscious mind, it was good. It was designed to allow the conscious part of our minds to remain free to analyze new data. But programmed with the world's negative thinking, our subconscious minds can become a liability instead of an asset.

RENEW THE SPIRIT OF THE MIND

You can be a positive person and yet have a negative spirit of the mind. Again, let me say that I am using the term *spirit* in the abstract sense of attitudes and ways of thinking. For example, the "spirit of America" is what we call Americanism, or a way of thinking that is peculiar to the people of this country.

Let's look at a difference between the spirit of the mind and the subconscious. I sometimes call the subconscious part of the mind "the robot mind" because it is totally programmed to trigger actions reflexively. Your subconscious mind doesn't think. It only reacts according to preprogrammed information. The spirit of the mind is the overall attitude you have toward life, and it is made up of all of the separate little programs you learned by your teen years.

If those attitudes have been basically negative, you will have a negative mind-set. You tend to see the worst in everything and in everyone. We call people like this pessimists. Others seemingly see through rose-colored glasses and are just as unrealistic. We call those people optimists. Most of us fall somewhere in the middle of these two extremes. We're optimistic about some things and pessimistic about other things.

So in order to change, you must realize that you do have a spirit of your mind, or a certain overall way of thinking. I'm not talking about spiritual matters or a "mystical" sort of thing. I'm talking about the very practical, everyday mechanics of the way your mind works.

As I have said, if you don't change the spirit of your mind after you're born again, the present mechanics of your mind will continue to operate just as they were programmed to years ago. No matter how many books you read or sermons you hear, you will still be the same. No matter how hard you try to change, you will be the same until the spirit of your mind is renewed to the image of Christ.

CHANGING THE MIND-SETS OF THE ISRAELITES

Remember how the nation of Israel was set free from Egypt and the bondage of Pharaoh? Supernaturally led by God, they crossed the Red Sea and walked through the wilderness on their way to the Promised Land. Oh, what exciting days those were! They were no longer slaves. They no longer had to make bricks for the Egyptians. They no longer had to eat leeks, garlic and live off the fleshpots. They were delivered and set free. They could at last have the life they had dreamed about. God was working on their behalf.

But as they headed toward the Promised Land, they began to run into problems. First, there was no water. But rather than thinking that God could provide water, they said, "We want to go back to Egypt. We miss our old lifestyle. We would rather be slaves than be out here in this wilderness." But when God did provide water, the spirit of their minds didn't change.

A few days later, they ran into another problem. God provided fresh food every day, but they began to murmur again. They wanted meat. So

God provided all the meat they could want until most of them couldn't stand any more. (Ex. 16,17.)

Every time the Hebrews murmured against God in the wilderness they had one main "programmed" thought, an operative phrase, that came out of their mouths. It was, "I wish we had stayed in Egypt!"

That phrase gives us a clue as to the state of their minds. They had lived in Egypt four hundred years. The customs, fashions and culture of that country had become theirs. They had lived in bondage for the last part of that period. And the Israelites whom Moses led out had been slaves all of their lives. So they had a slave mentality, *a state of mind* that caused them to feel uncomfortable with freedom. They had grown accustomed to depending on the Egyptians for their provisions. The spirit of their minds was negative. They were used to grumbling and complaining.

So even though God had promised them many good things, the only way they could handle difficulties in the meantime was to grumble and murmur against the One in authority. And they did this despite God's many miraculous signs.

They finally got to the border of the Promised Land in spite of their rebellion and disobedience. There they looked over into the land of Canaan, the land which flowed with milk and honey. When the twelve spies returned from their reconnaissance mission into Canaan, apparently only two of them had allowed God's dealings with them in the wilderness to renew the spirit of their minds. The two were Caleb and Joshua. They were the only two spies who saw the land clearly and could believe that God would continue to do in the future what He had done for them over the past two years.

The other spies grumbled and complained, "There are giants over there. They're too big for us, too powerful. We will never be able to inhabit the land. Moses has brought us out here just to destroy us. This is too hard. Let's go back to Egypt!"

Most of us are appalled when we read this account in Numbers 13 and 14. Yet we operate the same way today as the Israelites did then.

The Israelites' thinking controlled their behavior, and they got exactly what their minds were programmed for—defeat and destruction. Was it God's will for them to waste their lives in the wilderness? Was it His will for a delay of another thirty-eight years before the Israelites occupied the Promised Land? No, but as they thought in their hearts, so they were. (Prov. 23:7.)

God could get the people out of Egypt, but He couldn't get Egypt out of the people. The spirit of their minds defeated them. God could deliver them from Egyptian bondage, but He couldn't deliver them from the bondage of their minds. Why? Is He not all-powerful, all-knowing and omnipresent? Yes, He is, but He won't override the freedom of choice that He created in man. If He did, He would be forcing His will and His choice on us. God abides by His own principles, terms and limits that He has established for man.

God solved the Israelites' situation with a very interesting answer. He told them that everyone who was twenty years old and younger would enter the Promised Land. Everyone older than twenty would die in the wilderness—except for Caleb and Joshua, who would become their new leaders.

Apparently, the older you become the more you tend to have your mind set in such a way that it becomes very difficult to change. Most people simply will not change. They would rather die than admit they need to change. So, most people don't change after they reach a certain age.

Younger people have it much easier. They are more open to change, and it is easier to renew the spirit of their minds. There seems to be a point—after a pattern has been repeated over and over—that our thinking becomes almost set in concrete. After a certain way of thinking is established long enough, it becomes a stronghold—an area of your mind, fortified by custom, which is set against change. Any change then appears to be a threat, and your defense mechanisms go into operation against change to protect the status quo.

But it is important to remember that *there is no limitation on change set by God after a certain age.* You don't have to accept the old adage about not being able to teach old dogs new tricks. It *is* possible to change thought patterns at any age. The "lever" to pry out the old and replace it with new is how badly you desire to change it.

My question to you is this: Are you a wilderness grumbler? And if you are, do you really want to renew the spirit of your mind? Or would you rather hang on to old thinking and linger in the wilderness? Be honest now. Do you want to go into a new, abundant, promised land, or would you rather die in the wilderness? Do you want to be part of the majority who would rather die than change? Or are you willing to give up your past ways for God's ways of thinking?

If you are willing to change the spirit of your mind, you can stop being a slave to your old thoughts and begin to prosper. If you are willing, you can leave Egypt behind and start living in your promised land. But to do that, the spirit of your mind must change.

The spirit of your mind affects your physical body as well as your behavior, attitudes and actions toward others. In Proverbs 17:22, the Word says that a merry heart does as much good for you as medicine does, but a broken spirit will cause your bones to dry up. If your heart—the spirit of your mind—is positive and happy, then your physical body will be stronger and healthier. But if your heart is negative, pessimistic and always seeing the bad, your physical body will "dry up."

I knew someone who went through this kind of thing. In fact, she had an image of a God who was mean and brought bad things into her life. She thought that He was part of her problem. She believed He caused her to be sick so she could develop spiritually and become more compassionate. And that negative spirit of her mind caused her body to manifest physical symptoms. Her bones in essence dried up. She developed rheumatoid arthritis, and her joints became stiff and fragile. Very soon, she was stiff, pain-ridden and greatly depressed. Because I knew her well, it was easy for me to trace the cause of her physical problem to the condition of her mind. The spirit of her mind was corrupted and negative.

I saw another example of how the mind affects our physical well-being in a young boy whom my family lived near when I was a child. My brother and I grew up around horses and cattle. We were rambunctious little critters ourselves. When we left the house in the morning, we could end up anywhere on the ranch. We could end up riding horses or steers, walking fences or making tree forts.

Our parents never worried about us too much. But our neighbor boy's family was very concerned over him. They constantly watched him, guarded him and protected him. They worried over the least little thing. They were afraid to let him play in the field because he might fall down. They were afraid to let him climb a tree because he might fall out of it. He was smothered.

Before he was out of his teen years, my childhood friend died. No one was exactly sure what killed him; it wasn't a disease or a condition. I personally believe he died from being smothered to death. I can't prove it, but I watched his parents' fearful, negative state of mind smother him—eventually, in my opinion—to death.

So again I ask you: Do you really want a new life? Or do you want to just continue on with what you've had for years and years? Discover your net worth, and the key to changing your thinking is yours.

KEYS TO PERSONAL APPLICATION

"Preprogrammed thoughts control
our lives more than we may ever know."

1. What behaviors in your life have you been unable to change?

   _____

   _____

2. Why did Israel wander forty years and not receive its inheritance?

   _____

   _____

3. How have your physical health and strength been affected by the spirit of your mind?

   _____

   _____

Many people want change—but only if it can happen "right now." But change isn't defined or confined by time. *Change is a process* that must continue if the desired result is to be reached. *Change* is a lifestyle that we adopt and begin to function in for the rest of our existence.

Renewing the spirit of the mind isn't easy, yet it is something everyone can do, and it will produce lasting change. I think by now you have seen that I'm not trying to sell you some quick-fix scheme or some simplistic program to follow.

You know what I'm talking about. For example, look at diet programs. If you fast or take certain drugs, you might lose a lot of weight in a few weeks. But you know how that turns out. The same eating habits that put the weight on in the first place will cause you to gain it back very soon. But when you change your thinking about food, you can change your eating habits, and the results will be lasting.

Your subconscious, reflex-thought system—what I call the "root" of the mind—is the system under the surface which isn't seen, but controls what happens in your life.

So with this in mind, let's take another look at Proverbs 23:7: **As he** [a man or woman] **thinks in his heart, so is he.** This could be paraphrased this way: As the spirit of your mind is, so your conscious mind is; and therefore all of your life is. If your heart is filled with negativity, then your life will be filled with it also. We must let Jesus help us change our hearts so our lives can change.

The spirit of your mind is like the foundation of a great skyscraper. The depth of the foundation dictates its height, and what is underground controls what can be constructed above ground.

This is exactly what the spirit of your mind does: It controls what is manifested in your life. The spirit of your mind controls your attitudes and ultimately all of your actions. This core of your thinking process isn't rational or reasonable because it doesn't contain the reasoning faculty of your mind. That is in the conscious mind. Ideally, we would reason things out, find the truth and the good about everything in our conscious minds, then file the truth away as a program to trigger or control our behavior.

But in the environment in which we live, this isn't possible. The best we can do is change the negative information we've filed away so we can operate on the correct program.

Now I want to show you how to recognize when you are operating from negatively stored information so you can change the abundance of your heart to thinking based on the principles of God. (Matt. 12:35.)

It Isn't Necessarily True

First, you need to understand that what is in your subconscious isn't necessarily true. It doesn't have to be true for the spirit of your mind to believe it and act on it. Many people do things that are totally irrational and unreasonable. But that is the way they learned to think, so they continue to act on those negative programs.

Look at how many Americans have credit problems and how the majority of people handle their finances. Is it reasonable? No. But it is the prevailing spirit of the mind in this country, so most people continue to handle money unwisely. Before World War II, the spirit of the mind in finances was to not owe anything. The credit syndrome really began after the 1940s, and it continues to flourish, even though it is an unreasonable way to handle money.

Look at abusive parents. Most of them know child abuse is irrational, irresponsible and wrong. Yet they continue to do it because most of them were abused themselves. Their programming that says *children are to be abused* is written heavily in their subconscious minds. That false, negative program controls their actions, although they don't want to be abusive.

THE SEVEN DS OF MIND RENEWAL

Remember, I love simplified steps, because they make action direct and easy. So here are seven Ds to help you further in the process.

D1: DECIDE
MAKE A DECISION TO CHANGE

It takes a decision to start the process of change. Being tired of your life or circumstances isn't enough. Not wanting or liking the way things in your life are will not cause you to change them. Most people have more than one thing in their life that they do not like, yet they will probably never do anything about it. You must *make a decision to change,* to go to a new place in life, to become a new person.

The decision to change is not like going on a diet or trying a new exercise program. Those are short-term trials, this must be a lifestyle and lifetime decision. If you don't truly want to change it will be too hard and you'll give up along the way. You can't do it because your spouse wants you to; you must want it. When you make a real decision for yourself, you are on your way to a renewed life.

D2: DESIRE
POSSESSING A STRONG DESIRE TO CHANGE

The second D step in the mind renewal process is *possessing a strong desire to change.* You will never change because someone else desires it for you. Neither will simply admitting your need for change actually change you. It takes a strong desire, a determination to change.

Knowing you need to change may affect some of your external things, but your basic internal thoughts won't change. Changing the external without changing the internal will only be a cosmetic change, like putting makeup over blemishes.

For example, say you know you need to drive within the speed limit and you make an effort to do so. But if you slip, you remind yourself by saying, "I am going to stay within the speed limit, because I know I need to." You have to make yourself do that day after day. You have to consciously think about not letting your foot get a little heavy, and you have to keep an eye on the speedometer. But if you changed the spirit of your mind from running at your own speed to running at the legal speed by *desiring* to stay within the limit, you would exchange one control program for another. You would automatically always stay within the speed limit, without having to consciously think about it all of the time.

Many times, in our family or marriage relationships, we do what we ought to do, but our actions and attitudes never become a desire. We are constantly having to force ourselves to do what is right, but we never enjoy it. This is why many divorces occur. We do things because we ought to, not because we want to.

Finally, doing what we ought to do finally gets to be more trouble than it is worth. But if we know how to change the spirit of our minds from a "duty" performed against our will to a desire to make the marriage work and make our spouse happy, divorce would almost never need occur.

Desire is the motivation of life. What one desires will ultimately drive them. Desire is what moves people to pursue goals and achievements over the long term. So build a desire for the things of God's Spirit into your mind—don't just live by "shoulds," or "need tos."

How do you build desire? You begin by wanting to want to do something. You might say, "I don't really *want* to lose weight, but I know that I should." If you operate with that thinking, you won't lose weight. And even if you did, you'd gain it back again.

Or you might say, "I don't want to change my spending habits, but I know that I should." But this kind of thinking won't bring permanent changes into your finances.

The way to change the spirit of your mind is to change the "I ought to" to "I want to" by beginning to say—if you want to lose weight, for example—to yourself, *I want to have a desire to change my eating habits.* Then before long, you will have the desire, and you can begin to say, *I want to change my attitude about food.* Then you will begin to see lasting results. You will no longer have to think about overeating. Your eating will be controlled by a positive program in the spirit of your mind.

So the second step in renewing the spirit of your mind is to possess a desire to change.

D3: *DEEPEN*
DEEPEN YOUR KNOWLEDGE BASE

The third D in the mind renewal process is to *deepen your knowledge base* of yourself and your world. Your knowledge base must increase if your life experience is to increase. Your knowledge base is the foundation on which you are building. But if your knowledge base is shallow or small, your life experience will be shallow or small.

Scientists say we use, at the maximum, about 10 percent of our brain capacity. If we expand the use of our conscious minds, that expands the subconscious, and our awareness of the potential within us will be greater. We expand awareness of opportunities and what life can be. Then we begin to seek after those things we have struggled to attain.

If your mind is so limited that you don't even realize what is available in life and what your potential is, then you will never strive for those things. So here are six ways to deepen your knowledge base:

1. Correspondence courses

2. Books, tapes and videos

3. Local programs, such as community colleges and seminars

4. Church classes

5. Private research in libraries

6. Job-training opportunities

There are literally thousands of correspondence programs that can be studied in your home, and there are many more thousands of books, tapes and videos available. If you simply spend a couple of hours a day reading, listening to tapes or watching videos, you can gain accurate, positive and effective knowledge. This can be done a few minutes at a time throughout the day as you are preparing for work, driving to the grocery store and so forth.

Attending local educational programs, seminars and conferences does take more time, but if you will spend that time, it will be well worth it. You will gain knowledge of people, information about current events and knowledge of spiritual things.

Most people live within a short distance of some public library. Become a member, and learn how to use the facilities that are free to everyone. A librarian will be glad to show you how to use the computer card indexes and even how to do basic research. Get a notebook for each subject. You might start with something that is of great interest to you. Spending an hour or so once a week or every two weeks is something most of us can find time to do *if we really have a desire to deepen our knowledge base.*

Finally, if your company is offering training sessions, take advantage of them, even if they aren't in your specific area of work. You will very seldom find that any knowledge you have gained is wasted. Any way that you can deepen your knowledge base will enable you to grow and change.

Remember, the spirit of your mind was well established during the first fourteen or fifteen years of your life. That is when most people stop learning. They may expand existing knowledge, but comparatively few people deepen their knowledge after that age. Most college work, for example, simply expands things already known. A small percentage of college work presents completely new knowledge.

If you force yourself to deepen your knowledge base, you will soon have a desire to learn, and that will affect the spirit of your mind.

D4: DILIGENCE
DILIGENTLY APPLY THE TRUTHS YOU LEARN

The fourth D in the mind change process is to *diligently apply the truths you learn* day after day after day. You change or renew the spirit of your mind through diligence.

- Diligently think new thoughts.

- Diligently seek new ways.

- Diligently apply yourself to grow and to change.

Most people fail in the process of mind renewal because they fail to be consistent in this fourth step. They don't constantly affirm the changes, so they don't persevere. You may think that saying or affirming something is vain—and it is if the words are empty, with no belief behind them. But by diligently speaking out loud your desire to change, your desire will build faith.

Romans 10:17 says, **Faith comes by hearing, and hearing by the word of God.** Sometimes in Christian circles we hear this verse quoted, "Faith comes by hearing and hearing and hearing and hearing." This is true, because hearing yourself say these changes is part of the process of building your faith. And when you stay diligent, changes can occur that make it possible for you to alter your attitudes and behavior.

As I said in the beginning of this chapter, renewing the spirit of your mind isn't an overnight plan. It is a lifetime plan. Renewing your mind is a lifestyle in itself, and to achieve your purpose, you must be diligent.

There is a saying that illustrates this concept. It goes, "The only way you can eat an elephant is one bite at a time." Likewise, the only way you can renew your mind is one bite, or one change, at a time. You must stay with the process day after day after day. It took a number of years to build your subconscious, so it may take years to renew it, taking one change at a time.

People spend half their lifetimes developing negative habits. Then suddenly one day they want to change them overnight. But it doesn't work that way. You built the spirit of your mind as a daily process, and you must renew it as a daily process.

If you want to see results immediately, the renewing process won't work for you. But if you will be diligent, I guarantee that you will see changes occur.

D5: *DEFEND*
DEFEND YOUR MIND AGAINST THE OLD THOUGHTS

The fifth D in the mind renewal process is *to defend your mind against the old thoughts,* the old attitudes and the old behaviors that once controlled you. You must constantly defend your new state of mind against your old ways of thinking and against limitations people want to place on you.

Just because you desire to change old thinking to new ways of thinking doesn't mean the old ways will automatically "fall off." Those old habits and ways of thinking will resurface time after time, sometimes for years. The tendency will be there to slip into the old bad attitude, the old sharp tongue, the old desire to just give up and throw in the towel. These kinds of old thoughts are like deep roots that keep popping up. Even if you pour a slab of concrete over them, they will creep through a crack in the concrete and resurface.

So you must always be ready to defend yourself against old thinking patterns. Defend your mind. Defend your thoughts against those old attitudes that come back to you. You also need to understand that just because old thinking patterns keep trying to pop back up doesn't mean that you haven't changed. Their resurfacing doesn't mean you aren't making progress. When those old ways of thinking resurfaces, you never want to give in to them and say, "I've been working on this for so long. I've been trying to change this for so long, but it doesn't seem I am making any progress."

Just keep on going, and put those old thoughts aside one more time. Every time you defend your mind against that old way of thinking, you strengthen the new way. Every time you allow the old thoughts to come back, you weaken the new way.

If you don't defend yourself, the old thoughts will come back, and you will find yourself going through the routine so many Christians put themselves through: change for two weeks and then back to the old. We tend to get excited over the latest new program, diet, tape, message and for a couple of weeks, we get all fired up. We're really going for it! Then suddenly, we find ourselves back in the same old habits and routines. Instead of being diligent about changing, we go looking for another new diet, tape or program.

How do you defend yourself against the old thoughts? You develop reminders for yourself. When you have had a way of thinking for a period of years, you can be overtaken by it before you realize it. You may have had a bad habit of using a sharp tongue toward your family or fellow employees. You must realize that there is a way of thinking that goes along with a sharp tongue and a bad attitude. That way of thinking begins long before the words are spoken.

But you can stop yourself from saying sharp words. Proverbs 30:32 tells us if we have an evil thought, we can put a hand over our mouths: **If thou hast done foolishly in lifting up thyself, or if thou hast thought evil, lay thine hand upon thy mouth** (KJV). So it can be done.

Now you have set a defense mechanism in your conscious mind: *As soon as I recognize a negative thought, I won't speak it. I will cast down that invalid thought.*

D6: *DISASSOCIATE*
DISASSOCIATE FROM THE PAST

This D step in the mind renewal process is an area that most people don't like to hear about: *Disassociate from the past.* You may feel comfortable with some of your old ties, but you may never get to the place that God wants to take you. Many of us want to hang on to longtime relationships in spite of the fact that they aren't beneficial; in fact, they are often detrimental. There are people in your life from whom you must dissociate yourself if you want to change.

If you continue in the same old relationships, you will continue with the same old lifestyle. But if you want a new lifestyle, you must take the fifth step: Create a new circle of friends.

When I decided twenty-five years ago that I was going to have a completely new life, I had been an average young American. I enjoyed smoking pot, drinking beer and going to parties. I went to work and got my paycheck, but I also wanted to have a good time. I enjoyed "getting loaded" and having different girlfriends. I liked driving my car with fancy "mags" and being what I thought was cool.

I was into the hip scene, snorting cocaine like everyone else I knew and just having a good old time in the way so many people do today. I didn't have a drug problem or a drinking or smoking problem; I had a lifestyle problem.

You don't stop snorting cocaine or drinking or even smoking cigarettes by dealing with the drugs, alcohol or tobacco. You have to deal with your lifestyle. The attitudes that allow you to enjoy that kind of life must be changed.

As for me, my ultimatum—serve time, or go into drug rehab— certainly helped me in the process. But you know, I could have chosen to serve the time and avoided my need to change. But I wanted to change. So when I said, "I'm going to change," I got involved with people who could teach, train and help me develop a new lifestyle. Soon I realized that the development of this new lifestyle meant I was going to have to develop a whole new circle of friends, because the people I had been hanging out with for so many years weren't thinking about changing. They weren't interested in doing anything different with their lives.

Every time I was with them, I was pulled back into the old habits, back into the old ways. If I talked to them about changing, they took it as a put-down, a criticism. I wasn't welcomed if I wanted to talk about change and becoming a different person.

Eventually, I had to dissociate myself from them, and it was difficult. I really didn't want to, because they were my friends, my old buddies. We had been together since high school. We had done so much together. I cared about them, and they cared about me. Yet I realized that if I wanted a renewed spirit of mind and a new lifestyle, I would have to leave my old friends. And you, too, will have to accept the fact that your desire to change will separate you from some old friends. You will have to develop a new circle of friends.

The truth about the matter is that most people in your life will resist your changing lifestyle. Some will embrace it, but others won't. There were many people I knew who would rather have had me using drugs, drinking beer and throwing away my money, than to have me create a new life and begin to prosper and enjoy myself.

Why did they feel that way? Because they resented what was happening to me—*and* because they didn't want to change. They wanted to stay the way they were, and the contrast with my new lifestyle made them uncomfortable.

The old adage is true: "Misery loves company." So get some new friends—friends who are going where you're going.

Jesus said in Matthew 10:34-37

> "Do not think that I came to bring peace on earth. I did not come to bring peace but a sword. For I have come to set a man against his father, a daughter against her mother, and a daughter-in-law against her mother-in-law; and a man's enemies will be those of his own household.

> "He who loves father or mother more than me is not worthy of Me. And he who loves son or daughter more than Me is not worthy of Me."

So the sixth D in the mind renewal process is *disassociate* from every relationship that does not enhance your walk with the Lord.

D7: DEPEND
DEPEND ON GOD AND OTHERS FOR SUPPORT

Renewing the spirit of your mind isn't something you can do by yourself. This process must be done with the help of the Holy Spirit, or it will not work. So the seventh D in the mind renewal process is to *depend on God and others for support.*

You aren't a hermit or an "island unto yourself." You need God, and you need friends! You can't change yourself by yourself. So build a support base. Believe that God wants your life to be blessed. He isn't part of your problem; He is your answer. He isn't trying to keep the good things of life from you. He wants you to be blessed. So always depend on Him to provide and make a way for you.

So far as your support group is concerned, every believer is an individual part of Christ's body. Whether some of us want to admit it or not, it's true. (1 Cor. 12:12-27.) And just as in the physical body, one part can do little without the other parts. You can glide into church services, and then glide out just as fast. Or you can nourish the other members as a strong and effective body part. If you separate yourself from other parts of the body, you will accomplish little, enjoy little and go without the life you desire. But once you choose to connect with other members, you yourself are nourished while you are nourishing others, and everyone gets blessed.

Perhaps you've heard yourself saying, "I'm going to be my own person. I don't need anybody. I'm going where I want to go. I'm going to do what I want to do. I will be free and independent." But what that really means as a Christian is that you are committing to a life of bondage to loneliness and isolation. So this seventh step is a very important one.

The seven Ds of decide, desire, deepen, diligence, defense, disassociation and dependence are lifestyle-changing choices you make every day. Choices require action. So in the next four chapters we will move from instruction to training. We will move from the academic knowledge of changing the spirit of your mind to the experience of actually doing it. Once you believe you can change, you can change!

KEYS TO PERSONAL APPLICATION

"The thoughts and attitudes you carry may not be
reasonable or rational, but they do control your life."

1. What negative things do you do even though you consciously realize
    you shouldn't?

    _____

    _____

2. Do you feel a real desire to change or do you feel outward pressure
    telling you that you *should* change?

    _____

    _____

3. What specific things do you do to deepen your knowledge base?

    _____

    _____

4. Are there relationships you may have to give up before you can change?

    _____

    _____

20

BELIEVE THAT
YOU CAN CHANGE

In this chapter, you will be writing in your notebook. I also suggest that you read this in a quiet place where you can meditate on what you read.

You have already seen how your thinking controls the way you act, which ultimately controls the way you live. The way you believe or think controls the way you are. Therefore, the way you see yourself determines what you will do with your life.

Remember, it doesn't matter to your subconscious control center if what you think is true or false. Once you have believed something about yourself, that is filed away in your subconscious as truth whether it is or not. So if you believe a thought, it becomes "true" in your life, whether or not it is reasonable or rational.

By renewing the spirit of your mind, you renew your whole life. By changing the way you think about yourself, you change the way you deal with your life.

STRENGTHS AND WEAKNESSES

By now I hope you have discovered your true image in Christ. We have discussed the glorious process through which you are changed. But sometimes, a "golden calf" or two will try to crawl up on the altar of your mind. You've already considered your mental net worth in both positive and negative thoughts. Now I want you to be completely honest in considering your own strengths and weaknesses.

- How do you esteem yourself at this time?

- What is the value you have placed on yourself?

It is very important to begin renewing the mind with an understanding of the way you see yourself. *Strengths* are the talents, qualities, characteristics and abilities that come naturally to you, the things you do without really trying. We all have areas where we are strong. Perhaps you're a strong communicator or a strong listener; perhaps you're good at doing things with your hands; maybe you're good at planning, organizing and administrating.

At the same time, everyone has areas of *weakness,* things that don't just flow naturally for you. You might like to do those things, but you can't—or at least you can't without great effort. For example, perhaps you always wanted to be musical, but you just aren't.

Now, I want you to take a moment and write down five of your strengths, five areas where you are strong, or five talents. Then write down five weaknesses. Take time to really think about these ten things, and be honest. Don't just skip over this, because listing these things will establish how you value yourself at this time. I'm not talking about what the Word has to say about you or how God lovingly values you. This exercise has to do with how *you* value *you.* So please take the time to be honest and thorough.

Write on a sheet of paper, "Strengths" on the top left and "Weaknesses" on the right. Now, take some time to fully consider and write them all down. Then we can move on and do some changing from where you are right now. Once you have completed this, I am going to ask you some important questions.

Now that you've completed the exercise, I want to talk to you about what you have just done as if I were a counselor sitting with you face to face. Let me ask you a few questions:

Was this difficult for you to do or relatively easy? If it was difficult, it could be that you don't really know yourself. Perhaps you've never taken the time to look at the things you do well. If weaknesses were easiest for you to list, then your thinking has been programmed predominantly with the things you do wrong or don't do well. You have focused on those instead of your strengths.

This is something you need to make a decision on right now. You need to *choose* to focus on your strengths, the things that are going to move you forward in life. Your weaknesses aren't going to cause you to prosper. Your weaknesses won't cause you to build a good marriage or a good family.

Focus on the strengths. Say this out loud: "I will focus on my strengths." Say it again: "I will focus on my strengths!"

FOCUS ON THE STRENGTHS

In previous chapters, we have talked about rejecting your old thoughts. In order to see those weaknesses turned around and made into strengths, it is necessary to reject them from your life.

For example, if you're a quiet person, you may think that is a weakness because you don't communicate. You may feel inadequate because you don't come out of yourself and share with others. However, as you examine your life and make these decisions, that "weakness" can be changed.

Begin to think about yourself as a good listener, not a bad communicator. Instead of thinking of yourself as quiet and shy, begin to think of yourself as someone who is able to listen. People who really know how to listen are rare. A good listener can learn more than a person who talks all the time. A good listener can know people and empathize with them.

Maybe you've always thought that you weren't very smart. You don't believe your mental capabilities are up to snuff with other people. If this is so, I want you to begin to see that changing. If you're a hard worker, you need to see that you can accomplish your goals in life through hard work—and many times, hard work will accomplish more and get you further than having high intelligence. So don't concentrate on the weaknesses. Turn them into strengths, and begin to say to yourself, *I'm not a slow learner. I'm not dumb. I'm a hard worker.*

Now, using the principles I've shown you on how to turn weaknesses into strengths, write down five positive responses, or five positive ways your weaknesses could be viewed. You don't have to figure out all the details or be specific. Above all, don't let negative thinking tell you, *This isn't going to work. It isn't going to make a bit of difference. I have always been dumb, and I always will be dumb.* Remember, we're getting rid of those old thoughts.

Finding ways to turn your perceived weaknesses into strengths will begin to renew the spirit of your mind about yourself. It will help you to begin to reject those weaknesses.

Negative Is as Negative Does

Another thing to remember is that those who focus on their own weaknesses probably focus on the weaknesses of others as well, and this is the beginning of relationship failure. Focusing on the negatives of life produces a very judgmental person. And no one likes to be around judgmental people. So those who want relationships that are prosperous and strong need to focus on their own strengths as well as the strengths of other people.

Now, please think through your list and then write down five strengths to replace your weaknesses.

Now look at the five strengths you wrote down. Even if you thought you had no special talents, when you look for your good points, you will see things about yourself that you have overlooked. You do have special qualities and talents that others don't have. You are unique and special in many ways.

Look at each of those five strengths and imagine what you can do with each of them. For example, if you wrote down that you are a quick thinker, imagine what would happen if you developed that trait. You might be a valuable person in a public relations department or in handling complaints. You would also be very valuable in a busy office or a phone center where many calls and decisions must be made on the spot. With training and experience, you could become a very valuable person in that situation. Or you might work in a day-care center where there are many children and decisions must be made quickly concerning their care. The strength of quick thinking would be of great value.

Begin to think of areas where you would really shine if you could just use those strengths. Don't think small. Don't limit yourself. Look at the first thing you wrote down, stop reading and think about it for a few minutes. Picture yourself using that strength in various settings. Then go on to the next one and do the same.

Now that you have seen yourself using those strengths and doing the things that could be done with the qualities you have, begin to expand on or enhance those strengths and weaknesses turned strengths.

List all of the adjectives you can think of to describe the person you've just been writing about. Is that person sharp? Beautiful? Handsome? Quick on the feet? Fast and efficient? Effective? Prosperous?

What are the ways you would describe yourself if you weren't you but someone else? How would you describe yourself if you were doing everything that could be done with the qualities and characteristics that are unique to you? What would you call that person?

A THIRTY-DAY EXERCISE

Now, here is an assignment you can do for the next thirty days. Each day, take out that list of strengths and weaknesses you've made into strengths, and read them out loud to yourself. If you will do that every day for the next month, you will begin to focus on your strengths. Then you will begin to see yourself living with those strengths, using them and producing results in your life.

The result of the exercise will be your placing a new and higher value on yourself. Instead of focusing on your weaknesses, you will be focusing on the strengths that will enhance them. It will only take you a few minutes each day, but you will be reprogramming your mind. You will be renewing the spirit of your mind.

It is important to say positive things about yourself. Don't say the things that tear down and destroy your self-worth. Every time you say something negative, you are strengthening your weaknesses. You are hurting yourself. Every time you say something positive, you are strengthening your strengths. You are building and helping yourself.

Begin to say, "I can accomplish what I desire to do. I'm sharp. My mind is clear. When I do a job, I do it right, I do it fast and I do it well."

If you continue to say those things out loud, you will begin to believe them and they will begin to come true in your life. Hearing yourself say them will help you even more than hearing someone else say them.

When you do this, you will be taking responsibility for the way you are. Go back during this thirty-day period to review the Scriptures provided in various chapters along with the five Rs and seven Ds of change. When you add to this the coming Scriptures and chapter questions, you will be fully engaged in the mind renewal process. Remember the Ds? They are:

1. *Decide* you want to change.

2. *Desire* to change.

3. *Deepen* your knowledge base.

4. *Diligently* follow through with the exercises listed in this chapter. Don't give up.

5. *Defend* your mind against your old thoughts, old habits and old ways of thinking. Fight them off, and don't let yourself fall into the old routines.

6. *Disassociate.* Get away from people who would keep you in the old pattern, people who tell you that you can't change or who try to keep you from changing.

7. *Depend* on God and on positive people around you to help support you.

As you progress, you will find your list of strengths growing and your list of weaknesses shrinking. When your own self-evaluation improves, a new confidence will lift you into situations, relationships and opportunities you couldn't have imagined before.

KEYS TO PERSONAL APPLICATION

"Your self-esteem is a major controlling factor in your life."

1. Have you written five strengths and five weaknesses?

_____

_____

_____

_____

_____

2. What areas of your life or personality make you feel the best about yourself?

_____

_____

3. What areas of weakness would you like to change first?

_____

_____

21

Mental fitness, like physical fitness, is a major key to obtaining peace and prosperity in your life. To be fit is to be sound, healthy and able to cope with the pressures of life without ill effects. Many people haven't learned to deal with daily pressures, so they experience negative effects in their minds and bodies regularly. Doctors see millions of people who are experiencing sicknesses, diseases and psychological disorders because of the mental and physical pressures of everyday life.

Mental stress is reflected in anxiety, worry and arguing or fighting with those around us, and it usually is expressed to the ones closest to us—the ones we care about the most. Mental pressure also shows up as difficulty in sleeping, anger and frustration when facing simple everyday things such as traffic jams or long lines at the bank or grocery checkout counters.

Confusion and doubts about the future, one's ability to handle the children or other responsibilities are other symptoms of mental pressure. Still other symptoms might be desiring to get away and leave everything behind or not wanting to deal with things any longer.

Many times, divorces are the result of people's reaching a breaking point in dealing with stress. They think their marriage is the problem instead of realizing the problems are symptoms of mental and physical stress from other areas of life. People think getting a new spouse, a new job or moving to a new city will solve their problems. But "escape" only means exchanging one set of pressures for another.

Physical symptoms are often reflections of stress and pressure: headaches, back and neck aches, stomach problems, ulcers, chest pains, fatigue, shortness of breath and over-weight or underweight problems. These shouldn't be part of our lives! Yet they often are. So we need to deal with our mental and physical problems. We can have victory by going through some exercises to bring fitness to mind and body. Then we will enter a new phase of life that is much more exciting and fulfilling.

REARRANGE YOUR PRIORITIES

The first step to fitness is to take a look at your schedule. What have you committed yourself to? What is taking up your time? Determine your top priority by figuring out what you spend the most time doing. Very often, people aren't aware they have established priorities, so their time is absorbed with things they don't really want or need to be doing. If this is the case in your life, it won't take long before your priorities are out of kilter and your life is out of balance. Once you write out your list, you may just have to do some priority rearranging.

The first thing to do is to write down the present arrangement of your priorities. Do this by examining your schedule. Find out what you spend the most time doing, and put that at the top of the list. Then see what you spend the next largest amount of time doing; list that second, and so forth.

In looking at your list you may find that your job is number one— making money, getting a promotion, doing what the company demands that you do. Continue down the list and see what place your family has, what place God has and what place the exercise of mind and body have. If you will be honest with yourself and take time to do this, you will be on the way to developing mental and physical fitness.

Take some time now to do it.

Assuming that you, like I and most other people, do have some priorities out of place, the following four questions will help you recognize what areas in your life are out of balance.

1. Who is in control of your time?

2. Who decides what is a priority for you?

3. What must you change to reorganize your time and priorities?

4. What is hindering you from reorganizing your time and priorities?

Very often, we allow the boss or our jobs to become the controlling factors in our lives. Perhaps I should say that money is the bottom line for many of us. The need for finances controls our time, and our relationships with our spouse and children often suffer. We are more dedicated to making money than to anything else. Of course, we need money to live. But many times, men generally will say they are workaholics for the good of their families when, in reality, the wives and children would rather have fewer things and more of Dad's time and attention.

A lot of men realize their mistakes when it's too late—when the divorces are final, the heart attacks happen or failures of some other sort occur. It is only then, after the destruction, that many are forced into realizing that their priorities had been out of alignment.

So be honest with yourself in answering those four questions— especially number four: What is stopping you from reorganizing the priorities in your life? If it's your job, you may have to quit that job, because your life is more important than *making money*. If it's some other person or relationship you need to examine the situation and bring about the change that is necessary.

Now I want to give you six priorities, six Fs on which your schedule should be built. You can use these in a variety of ways, and of course, you should apply them to whatever works for you personally. It is a positive list that has been used by many successful people in every type of lifestyle.

Six Important Priorities

The first priority is Jesus and *faith* in Him. You must have a right relationship with God, and you must have your life built on a spiritual foundation. There are too many pressures and difficult circumstances to handle on your own. So your first priority must be your faith life.

The second priority is mental and physical *fitness*. You need time for the exercising of your mind and body. If you don't have time to care for your mind and body, you won't have time for your job or your family, and you may die young.

Number three is *family*. Before finances, before jobs and before other commitments of life, you must make time for your family. If you don't have a successful relationship with your husband or your wife, your life is very shallow. If you can't enjoy your children, your life is out of order. If you can't spend time with them as they grow up and enjoy those early school years, including the camping, walks and hikes, you are living a very shallow existence.

Number four is *fellowship*. This includes your relationships with other people and with people in your church. Having friendships and involvement with people is more important than having a savings account, a good position at the company, or high status in society. What good is high status without friends? What good is having a large bank account but no one to enjoy it with? So fellowship with other people is extremely important.

The fifth thing on the priority list of those who are successful is *finances*. It is important to make money and meet the needs of your family, but it shouldn't be the number-one priority. Making money must be viewed from the proper perspective of your life. Money can be a positive influence, a tool to accomplish things with, but it must always be kept in the proper perspective with everything else. If money becomes your first love, it becomes the **root of all kinds of evil** (1 Tim. 6:10). The

Bible doesn't say *money* is the root of all evil; it says *the love of money* is the destructive force.

The sixth priority on our list is simply having *fun*. The old saying, "All work and no play makes Jack a dull boy" is very true. Without fun and relaxation, your faculties become dulled. You don't "take time to smell the roses" or enjoy the world around you. You should enjoy the life God has given you and the friends He has placed around you. Maybe find a hobby, something you enjoy. Perhaps this can be combined with family activities.

So here they are, the six Fs of prioritizing:

1. Faith

2. Fitness (mental and physical)

3. Family

4. Fellowship

5. Finances

6. Fun

Compare these six priorities with your present priorities and see what changes you can make to get your priorities into the proper order. You may not be able to do this all at once, but you can begin to work on them one at a time.

THE BEGINNING OF MENTAL FITNESS

Once your priorities are in order, mental fitness can begin through the removal of worry, anxiety and doubt. As we have discussed, what happens in your mind controls what happens in your life. So in order to get your life re-ordered according to your new priorities, you must get negative thinking out of your life. And worry is one of the most negative forms of thinking there is. Worry is actually having faith that something bad is going to happen. Worry is *negative faith*.

Mental fitness begins with getting worry and other negative beliefs out of your mind. You may think you are a "natural" pessimist. But you weren't born a pessimist. You weren't born a worrier. You were born without a care. You were born with the capacity to believe good things were going to happen every day. You had to learn how to worry. But with help from parents or others around you, you trained yourself to worry.

Now write down in your notebook ten things you worry about. Go ahead and write out a heading: "Ten Things I Worry About." Don't take time to study or figure them out. Quickly and honestly write them down. Perhaps you worry about getting your bills paid, the condition of your company, your physical health, your weight, your children, your house and needed repairs and other concerns like these.

Now take a good look at those ten things and put a check mark by those over which you have some kind of control. Then draw a line through each one over which you have no control.

Take a few minutes and look carefully at those which you can do something about. Consider what you could do if you looked at those things objectively as solvable problems instead of chronic worries.

For example, if your house is a mess, how could you change your own habits and use of time? Could you get your family involved in helping? Could you cut expenses elsewhere and hire someone to clean? What could you do to keep your house clean every day, and how would you feel if it were that way?

If you are worrying about your weight, what could you do to gain or lose? Could you exercise more? Could you change your eating habits?

As you take each of the things you checked and analyze them in this way, you will turn negative things into positive ones, just as you turned weaknesses into strengths.

Next, take the things that are crossed out and erase them from your mind. If you need to, go back and reread the previous four chapters of this book to see how to remove thoughts from your mind. Use that information right now with the first worry you crossed out.

Maybe your worry is about the neighbors, the state of the stock market, bank interest rates or possibly even the weather. Whatever it is, I want you to say, "I take no thought about that!" Say it out loud again and again.

Now take a look at the rest of worries you can't do anything about and begin to replace those negative thoughts with positive ones. Say, "I take no thought about the neighbors, the stock market, bank interest rates or the weather!" and continue through each one on your list.

Go through that list twice, saying, "I take no thought" about each of them. It is important to do this, so stop reading and take the time to do it now.

Proper Mental Food

Mental fitness continues with the proper feeding of your mind. If you aren't feeding your mind, it will get weak just as your body will if it isn't fed. If you go for a day or two without feeding your body, you will begin to get tired and weak. If you fast long enough, your body will cease to function and you will die.

Many of us have had our minds on a fast because of a lack of "food" and training, and as a result they are weak and tired. So one of the first priorities in renewing the spirit of the mind is to get it in shape. We must use discipline to get our minds strong, active and healthy.

Mental fitness comes with proper feeding and exercising of the mind.

The first step in feeding your mind is to remove what I call space-out time. This is the time you waste mentally by watching hours of worthless television programs. This doesn't sharpen your mental capacity; it is a waste of mental energy and is space-out time. When a born-again, Spirit-filled Christian spaces out in front of the tube, he or she is acting no differently than the child whose mind is captivated by a video game or a children's program; the child is oblivious to what is going on around him and is just absorbing junk food into his mind.

Maybe the junk food you've been feeding your mind with isn't television. For you, it might be the radio, novels or magazines. But junk food is junk food. And in order to renew the spirit of your mind, you must break the junk food habit and get rid of space-out time. You must begin to control what is going into your mind and what you are doing with your mind.

Scheduling the feeding of your mind is as important as scheduling your lunch, your job activities and physical exercise. So prepare a simple schedule. Block out space-out time with mental nourishment, and you will see a change. If you don't plan to feed your mind, it will go into atrophy. Without the proper exercise, your mind will become so lazy that you won't be able to create or come up with the ideas, opportunities, thoughts, plans and knowledge necessary to succeed and prosper in life.

FOUR WAYS OF FEEDING THE MIND

The number-one way to feed the mind is to *read*. Read the Scriptures daily. Memorize them. I suggest that you write down the following verses to start memorizing and making a part of your exercise every day:

- Exodus 23:25
- Joshua 1:8
- Proverbs 4:12-13
- Isaiah 53:3-7
- Matthew 5:1-16
- Matthew 8:17
- John 15:7

- 1 Corinthians 13:1-8

- 2 Corinthians 10:4-5

- Ephesians 1:3; 2:1-10; 4:17-18

- Philippians 2:1-16; 4:19

- Colossians 3:1-24

- 1 Peter 2:1-2; 13-25

- 1 John 4:17; then one chapter of 1 John daily

With sixty-six books in the Bible, these are just a start. But they will give you the food needed to activate the spiritual appetite and needs of the spirit of your mind.

You will also want to make time in your schedule to read other published materials that will bring positive motivation into your life. There are many excellent books that aren't "junk food." There are many *good* books that will inspire you and cause you to grow. Don't waste time reading garbage. Read material that will help you in your field of endeavors and accents the possibilities of life.

Number two is *schedule time to listen.* Listen to cassette tapes that contain positive biblical and educational teaching material. Use the cassette deck in your car when driving, and schedule other times with a Walkman or home tape player to listen to teachers who move, stir, feed and challenge you. Also schedule video-viewing times, because there are many good videos you could watch instead of wasting time in front of worthless television shows.

Number three is *study.* Look for study materials that will help you in your field of work or with your family. If you are a parent, get some good books on parenting. For example, someone who wants to raise a dog to be an obedient and fun pet, will go out and buy a book on dog care, but many of us never bother to look for information on rearing our children, which is something of much greater significance.

Read books and then sit down with your spouse at least once a week and discuss what you have read. Study these materials. You might get a book on something your children are interested in, and start encouraging them to grow in it. Have a scheduled time with them and say, "Let's talk about this a little bit and see how we can get you where you want to be with it."

Number four is *use your imagination*. You have an imagination, whether you use it or not. Like I said earlier, some of us haven't been creative in so long that our imaginations are inactive. But you can stir up your imagination and begin to create new ideas and opportunities.

How can you improve the quality of your life? How can you improve your relationships? How can your job be different or better? Everything in this world began as a creation in someone's imagination first. You have a mind too, just like the inventors and innovators you may have admired in the past. Your mind can create in your own world, your own sphere of influence. You just have to take the time to imagine.

Also write down into your weekly schedule one way you can improve in each of these four areas.

PHYSICAL FITNESS TOO!

Being physically fit is as important as being mentally fit. In fact, your physical fitness controls the quality of your lifestyle. Overweight, tired and weak people can't do what they want to do. They can't live the standard of life they really want to live.

All of us tend to develop excuses, rationalizations and justifications about our not exercising. We tend to excuse ourselves until we get to the point that we are living far below the standard we want to have. If you will be honest with yourself, you will realize that when you are physically unfit, you can't live the life you really want to live. You can't do what you really would like to do. I'm not just talking about those who are overweight. Being underweight can hinder you just as much as being the right weight with out-of-shape, flabby muscle tone.

Here are some general questions you can answer regarding physical fitness:

- Why have you allowed physical weakness to develop?

- Why have you avoided exercise?

- Why have you allowed yourself to become easily fatigued and short of breath after physical activity?

I believe you will find that the answers to these questions fall into one of the following five categories:

- Are you lazy?

- Are you unaware of the situation?

- Are you harboring a "death wish" to the extent that you have just given up on life?

- Are you avoiding other people or circumstances?

- Are anger and frustration controlling you to the point that eating and retreating into sleep or becoming a "couch potato" are your tranquilizers?

If you are sincere about changing your present physical situation, you must be totally honest. You need to answer these questions objectively. If you will be honest about what has caused you to allow physical weakness to take over your life, you will be on the way to changing the situation and turning your life around.

Perhaps you've tried to change before and haven't been able to do so. In that case, what you need to find out is what caused you to fail. Like a lot of other people, you may have tried diets, started exercise programs, bought memberships to health clubs or gone through different programs to get your body in shape. If this describes you, see if the following list contains one or more of your reasons for failure:

- You never really tried to change, but just made a token attempt.

- You didn't persevere and only stayed at it for a week or two. Your attempts to change have never been consistent or long-term.

- Your environment, the people around you, made it too difficult. Peer pressure to not change kept you from changing.

- You never really felt a need to change, and never saw the benefits of becoming physically fit.

Again, be honest with yourself. Consider each of these possibilities and see if one of them is your underlying problem. If you really want to change, look at yourself until you see the reason that caused you to fail in previous attempts.

The next exercise is to confess that your weakness will no longer control you. Say, "Laziness won't control me," or "Unawareness of the problem won't control me," or "The desire to give up and die won't control me," or "Avoidance of the issue will no longer control me," or "Anger will no longer control me!"

CUT IT OUT—GET UP AND OUT!

There are two areas of physical fitness to deal with: eating nutritious food and choosing the right exercise program. There are so many books, tapes and information available on these subjects that I'm not going to try to give you a complete food or exercise plan. I will, however, give you some thoughts to help in the renewing of the spirit of your mind in these areas.

As you apply yourself to the diet or exercise programs you choose, you will begin to see results. But you must have the right thoughts and attitude before any program will work for you.

You can make your own program by writing down one thing you could do to improve your diet instead of revising everything you eat. Maybe cutting out coffee, sugar or salt would make a big difference in your life. Determine to deal with that one thing first. Go through the process of change that you learned in the first part of this book. Just remember, it will be your heartfelt desire to change that will give you the strength to overcome the habit and addiction.

Write down one thing you can do every day to improve your physical condition. You might want to start with a daily walk and a few simple exercises in your bedroom. Riding an exercise bike for five minutes might be a good choice for you. Just find one simple thing you can do to start becoming physically fit.

Get your calendar and write down those plans each day for the next thirty days. Then make yourself follow that plan. Don't think about whether you want to do it. Don't ask yourself if there have been any changes or results—just follow your plan! You will begin to see positive results after thirty days. You will find yourself feeling better and even looking better. This is the beginning of a physical fitness program that can make a tremendous difference in your life.

Make this your mental and physical fitness confession:

1. My priorities are in order: faith, fitness, family, fellowship, finances and fun.

2. My mind is free from worry and is growing in knowledge.

3. My body is getting healthier, stronger and more active every day.

As you apply yourself to these principles, the spirit of your mind in this area will begin to be renewed. By taking time to examine your life and plan changes, you will enter into a new realm of mental and physical fitness. You will begin to enjoy yourself and life in a much greater way.

KEYS TO PERSONAL APPLICATION

"Being mentally/physically fit will decide how
much of life you enjoy and how far you will go."

1. How much time do you spend worrying, anxious or upset about situations in your life?

   _____

   _____

2. In what condition are the schedule and priorities of your life?

   _____

   _____

3. What priorities of the six are out of order in your life?

   _____

   _____

   _____

   _____

   _____

   _____

22

I wrote earlier about putting too much time, energy and focus on finances. But of course we all know that finances are very important. So in this chapter, I want to give you some practical steps that will help you reach financial goals without overemphasizing the desire or search for money.

If you were granted three wishes, more than likely one of them would be for money. Hoping for wishes to come true, however, isn't realistic. Your financial stability can't be based on wishful thinking. What brings financial stability is exchanging poverty thinking for prosperity thinking.

The reason it is so hard for most of us to understand that financial prosperity is a way of thinking is that we are convinced that more money would bring happiness. Yet that is a lie which has so many people caught in a trap. More money isn't the answer to our problems, no matter how strongly we are convinced that it is. That is a fallacy.

Many of us have increased greatly in our incomes over the years, yet we are in the same condition we were in when our incomes were considerably smaller.

So having more money won't change your circumstances or solve your problems. The way you think about money will control the way you handle the money you have.

Here are four stories of people I know who prove this point.

RAY, JIM, FRANK AND BILL

Ray was raised in a nice home, went to college and got a degree in history which he never used. He began working in a drugstore as a teenager making $1.50 an hour. After twelve years, his salary had grown to about $6 an hour. With two children and a wife, Ray was poor—to put it simply. He had scraped enough money together to buy a small house in a poor section of town. Every month, he spent every dime making his house payment, keeping an old truck running, buying food for his family and just barely getting by.

Ray tried doing different things. In fact, he eventually went to work for one of the drug companies that supplied products to the store where he had first worked. Yet he was still just barely making ends meet. His salary had gone up to about $1,500 a month. "Barely getting by" was still his testimony.

Then one day Ray showed up at our church in Seattle and began listening to the teaching about renewing the spirit of the mind. He began to change the way he thought. That of course caused him to change on the job. He became a better worker, and his company offered him a better position—a higher paying job in another city. But by then he had become a part of our congregation. He was enjoying the teaching and changes he was experiencing and didn't want to move. So he turned down the job and went without work for two months.

Now, you might think, *Boy, Ray has gone from bad to worse. Here is a fellow who was poor. Now he has no job at all.*

But in reality, Ray was finally getting his priorities right. He was changing his thinking internally, and before long he would make some major changes externally.

Remember, when you begin to change, there may be some things from which you have to disassociate yourself. So Ray disassociated from his past and the people he had been involved with. Soon he was a part of a new staff and a new company, involved with a new position and making more money than he ever had before. Today he owns a brand-new home, drives beautiful cars and his income is in the top 10 percent of the whole nation. His wife and children are blessed. They are very prosperous people.

How did that all happen? Was it that he got a better education, a lucky break or an inheritance? No, what happened is that Ray changed his thinking. He learned who he was in Christ and made the great exchange that can only come through biblical mind renewal. And the Lord blessed Ray's life so he could be a blessing.

Now let me tell you about Jim. When Jim came to our church several years ago, he was more than $30,000 in debt. I'm not talking about debt from a house mortgage. I'm talking about consumer debt—credit cards and so forth. He didn't know where his money had gone. He had taken out loans and obtained credit cards from just about every credit union and store in town, yet Jim had nothing to show for it. He had hocked everything he could to pay off the bills. He even sold his house to try to catch up, but that didn't help much. Jim was in a very bad financial spot.

Soon the government took over his finances, garnished his wages and told him what he could spend his money on. Every month, his paycheck went to a federal court that distributed the money he made.

But Jim began to change his thinking and renew his mind. Within a short period of time—less than half the time the government had said it would take—he was completely out of debt and making more money than he ever had before. Things seemed to be going great.

But one thing hadn't happened. Jim hadn't completely renewed his mind. He had only changed a few ideas. So even though he was making twice as much as before, his debts soon began to grow again, just like some people who lose a few pounds and then gain the weight back. As soon as he realized what was happening, he began to renew his mind even more. He made a complete change, and his financial condition stabilized. His income didn't shoot up again, but Jim no longer had to struggle with the pressure of always being in debt.

The last two men I want to tell you about are still struggling with their financial affairs. They're not broke, but neither are they prosperous in the biblical sense. Maybe you know one of them.

I'm going to call the third man Frank. He is one of those people who always seems to have a good job with enough money. Yet at the end of every month, he has spent all he had. He isn't behind, but he has nothing left over. He didn't plan properly. He spent some money on fixing up his house and then borrowed even more to pay off the excess construction bills on the house. So for several years, his family has barely made ends meet from month to month. He has developed a lifestyle of barely getting by. For Frank, it wouldn't matter if his income increased $500 or $2,000 a month. At the end of the month, he would always be at zero.

The last person I want to tell you about I have named Bill. Bill had inherited a business and a large amount of money from his father, and he spent all his time trying to hang onto it.

When I got to know Bill, he had more than enough money, three cars in the garage and a beautiful waterfront home. Yet to hear him talk, he was about to go under at any time. He was constantly saving, guarding and protecting his money. He was making sure he didn't lose the money that had been left to him. He spent his days worrying that his friends might be trying to get his money. He has gone through two bad marriages, and he is working right now on the third. Even though Bill always has more than enough money, things are always tough. His greed and the fear of losing his inheritance are destroying his life.

I'm sure that you have seen similarities between these stories and your own financial situation. It isn't the *money* that has to change; it isn't the economic system that has to change; it isn't your boss, company or job that has to change. What needs to change is your thinking about money. Then and only then will your finances stabilize.

FIVE ATTITUDES OF A PROSPERITY MENTALITY

When you have the right mind-set and attitude about anything, money included, you make yourself a candidate for God's abundant best. So get ready to write again. Here is a checklist for your attitude. I want you to write down your thoughts on finances. But first, ask yourself these questions:

- Do I never have enough?

- Am I always trying to get more?

- Do I have to save every dime I get?

- Is my attitude, "Easy come, easy go"?

- Do I find myself often thinking, "If I could just get another loan, everything would be all right"?

Briefly, in two or three sentences, write down how you *think* about money. Is it a struggle to get or a struggle to keep? Is it a controlling factor in your life or a tool in life? Go ahead and write.

If you have written down all sorts of positive thoughts about money, but you have had financial difficulties in the past, you have just lied to yourself! Why? Because it is impossible to have positive thinking about money and be going through negative experiences. All of us may face tough times, but if your finances have been in bad shape for a long time, it may be due to some bad thinking. You must be honest with yourself and face the negative thinking you have about money and finances. Being honest with the way you think is the first step to making any kind of change.

Now, here are some Scriptures you need to add to your daily mind renewal commitment: God wants all of us to prosper financially and enjoy the good of the land. (Isa. 1:19.) God wants us to have enough to leave as an inheritance to our children (Prov. 13:22), to give to the poor (Deut. 15:7) and to sow into the work of the ministry. (Gal. 6:6.) To do God's will on the earth, we need to prosper financially, and He will help us reprogram our minds in this area so we can do it.

SEVEN MONEY CONCEPTS

Now, here are seven thoughts that can turn your financial thinking around. Speak them out loud until you believe them:

1. I can manage money. I can control it and use it properly. I'm not foolish with money. I don't waste it.

2. There is more than enough money available to me. I am not limited or held back by "the system." I'm not stopped by the past, by my education or by anything else.

3. I use money wisely, invest it wisely, manage it wisely, earn it wisely and save it wisely.

4. I can save money. It doesn't slip through my fingers. It isn't gone at the end of the week or the month. I save money. I pay myself before I pay the rest of the world. I can save money.

5. I'm growing in financial prosperity. I'm increasing monthly. I'm not struggling, I'm not barely making it and I'm not getting farther and farther behind. Every month, I increase.

6. The economy of this world doesn't control me. My job doesn't control my finances. My boss doesn't control my finances. The government doesn't control my finances. The IRS doesn't control my finances.

7. I'm a liberal giver. I enjoy giving. I enjoy giving to my friends. I enjoy giving to the poor. I love giving to ministries. I'm not selfish. I'm not greedy. I'm a liberal giver.

As you think and say these things and make them a part of your normal thinking, God will help you change your life. You will begin to find the opportunities necessary to turn your present financial condition around.

Six Ways to a Healthy Cash Flow

Remember, I love good, practical, simplifying steps, because they provide simple and direct battle plans to produce change in life. These next six steps will help you manage your money and will bring you into a pattern of growth:

1. You must know what your current financial condition is.

2. You must know where your money is going.

3. You must decrease your expenses to 80 percent of your income.

4. You must establish a monthly budget and follow it.

5. You must begin to save 10 percent.

6. You must begin giving 10 percent *and beyond,* if you don't already do this.

To work the first two steps, you may have to write down everything you spend for thirty days. We have found in our financial counseling that many people don't know how up to half of their money is spent. They shop at convenience stores, constantly eat out at fast-food restaurants and go down to the mall; and their money just sort of disappears. So you may have to write down every penny for thirty days to see what your situation is and where your money is going.

In order to get your expenses down to 80 percent of your take-home pay, you may have to cut back on grocery spending, recreation, clothes or other areas. But decrease that monthly expense however you can if you want to get your finances in shape.

MAKE YOUR PLAN AND THEN WORK YOUR PLAN

Next, make a plan. People who live "by the seat of their pants" usually don't have a clue of where they're going. They don't know where they are or even how they got there. So work out a plan for your finances. Set up a budget. A budget is simply a money plan.

Begin to save 10 percent. Pay yourself before you pay the landlord, the utility bills and everyone else. Save that money and only use it for very special asset-increasing investments—a new home, a car or special things.

Then start giving 10 percent tithes and offerings. Give to your church and other ministries. Money you give to the work of God is like seed sown in a field—the farmer knows he isn't going to reap a harvest until he plants some seed. Start planting *your* financial seed.

My wife and I have been able to increase what we give by more than 30 percent. Our goal is to eventually give up to 90 percent and live on 10 percent of our income. Think of the freedom, peace of mind and happiness that would come by knowing you are giving most of your income to help others while you are still living a comfortable, prosperous life. Be a liberal giver, and you will find great freedom in your finances.

As your personal worth increases, your finances will increase. When you do more than you are paid for, you will start getting paid more. When you are worth more than you are paid, you will start getting more pay. So the most important change in finances is increasing your personal value. Increase what you are worth to your company and to society around you.

Finally, I want you to take some time in completing this chapter by exercising your imagination. I want you to write down what you think you could be worth. Write down ten ways you could be worth more on your job or in your community. These decisions could include improving your self-discipline, your efficiency, the way you deal with your neighbors or the decision to get more education. As you increase your personal worth, be looking for new opportunities. Don't get stuck in that rut of a maintenance position. But as you increase in value, keep your eyes open for better jobs with better incomes.

At the same time, remember to keep your priorities in proper order. If your priorities get out of balance, all these other things won't work. Your life will get out of balance again, and you will begin to struggle.

As you change what you think and what you say, your financial situation will change to give you God's abundance and make you a blessing to others. Don't waste your life hoping for a break or some lucky event that will change your fortune. Jesus said, **"But seek first the kingdom of God and His righteousness, and all these things will be added to you"** (Matt. 6:33).

KEYS TO PERSONAL APPLICATION

"God wants you to prosper, but it must start in a right heart."

1. What do you really believe about money in your life?

   _____

   _____

2. Of the five prosperity attitudes, which one is the hardest for you?

   _____

   _____

3. Are you a tither?

   _____

   _____

23

We need to discuss one of the most important aspects of the successful Christian life: human relationships. Your relationships with others determine the activities of your life, the success and harmony of your marriage and the security and promotions you experience in your job. I would like to begin by giving a couple of examples of men I have worked with in the past.

The first man is Don. He was a good worker and very well-qualified. He was very efficient and knew how to do the job right. But his attitude was so bad that he never got along with others in the company, including management. He figured they were stupid and didn't know how to do things right. *If they would just leave me alone,* Don thought, *I could get it the job done better than any of them.*

So Don was constantly out of a job and looking for work, although he was one of the best in his field. Because of his poor relationships, he never moved up the ladder in the companies at which he worked. His relationships kept him from being promoted, and many times it cost him his job.

Another person, whom I will call Richard, is someone I spent some time with years ago. Richard was a very good student. He took extra classes and really studied for the job he was assigned to do. He worked well and never bothered anyone. In fact, he was happiest if you never talked to him and he never talked to you. He would just put his entire focus on his work while shutting out the rest of the world. He worked like that all day, every day.

He did a very good job, but he had little or no contact with those around him. He had some of the same problems as Don! If there was a cutback or a change in responsibilities, Richard was either the first to go or the last to be promoted. Because he wasn't involved with the people around him, fellow workers and management didn't know him. And when people don't know you, they don't trust you. Lack of relationships hindered Richard in his progress through life.

One of these men was hindered by developing bad relationships through bad attitudes; the other was hindered by developing no relationships at all.

I wouldn't have succeeded as well as I did in a number of jobs early in life if it weren't for good relationships on the job. Fellow workers with whom I had built relationships would help me in those areas in which I lacked experience or training. At the same time, management was able to believe that I had potential and would promote me because of good relationships. They felt they knew me and knew what I would and wouldn't do.

What is the condition of your relationships with those around you? Think about the people you work with, live with and associate with most often.

- Are your relationships rewarding and fulfilling?

- Are they weak, stagnant and boring?

- Are you excited to be around the people you know? Or do you just put up with them?

Remember, you can't change other people; but you can always change yourself. The beginning of a good relationship isn't to worry about what others are doing. You can make yourself a better friend, a better business associate or a better church member by building the qualities and characteristics for positive relationships into your own life.

So let's take a look at some steps you can take to build exciting, fulfilling and rewarding relationships with others. Here are six qualities that will serve to build strong relationships.

1. Be encouraging to others.

2. Be interesting.

3. Be exciting.

4. Be giving and generous.

5. Be honest.

6. Be there when they need you.

These characteristics will begin to make you the kind of person others want to be around. When you are that kind of person, you are on your way to experiencing exciting, fun-filled relationships.

FIVE LEVELS OF RELATIONSHIPS

Now I want to give you five levels of relationships that people experience in one way or another. And before we start, I want you to know that very few people go beyond level two.

The first level is *acquaintance.* We bump into some people now and then. We know their names and a little bit about them. When we see them, we make small talk. We shoot the breeze, talk about the weather, the job, the stock market, the latest television show or how our families are doing. We are simply acquainted with them.

The second level is a *working relationship.* We get along well in the workplace. We are with each other daily. We ask about the family and things having to do with work.

The third level is *friendship.* Friends are the ones you would give to. If they need $500 and you have it, you would give it to them without thinking twice about it, because you are good friends. Perhaps you travel together, sit and fellowship together or talk about things that you keep private from acquaintances.

The fourth level is *intimacy*. This is a *close* friend. On this level, you are willing to share any part of your life. You talk about problems you may be having with a spouse or a teenage son. You are willing to let them know your fears, hopes and dreams. There isn't a thing you would hide from someone with whom you have this kind of relationship.

The fifth level is *marriage* in a total union relationship the way God intended it to be. The marriage relationship is oneness. Your spouse knows everything about you, and you know everything about your spouse. There is nothing hidden, nothing covered up. You are able to discuss anything and everything. Your life is one with your spouse.

Now you can understand why I said most people never go beyond level two, even in their marriages. Many people don't even have friend-ships with their spouses.

Hindrances to Intimacy

If you are a level-two person, I want you to think about each of the following five reasons your relationships may be shallow. Be honest with yourself as to whether any of these reasons are keeping you from having good, satisfying relationships.

1. The feeling that you don't need intimate friends. You really don't want to share your life and be intimate with others. This view is all too common in society today.

2. You have a fear of others knowing the real you. You have the thought that if they really knew you, they wouldn't like you. So you pretend to be the kind of person you think they would like, and you end up being artificial and shallow.

3. Things in your past that you don't want others to know—perhaps an abortion, a bankruptcy, a past divorce, a business problem.

4. You think you don't have time for friends. You don't have time to talk, to get together with others. You're too busy. Other things are more important.

5. You wait for other people to reach out and be your friend. You wait for them to call, to set up the engagement. Waiting for others to take the first step is a great hindrance to intimacy in our relationships.

Now, take some time to look at yourself honestly. Review the major relationship hindrances I have listed below again; then write down any other reasons you may know of that keep you from making friends.

- Is it the feeling that you don't need friends?

- Is it a fear of others' knowing you?

- Is it because of past things you feel you must cover up?

- Is it not taking time to get to know people?

- Is it waiting for others to make the relationship work?

Add any other reasons that have hindered you in committing to relationships. Then start making some positive relationship decisions.

Decide that you are going to take the first step and begin to build positive relationships.

Decide that you aren't going to let your job and other activities steal from your relationships.

Decide that you are going to be bold and no longer afraid of people's getting to know who you are.

The risk of rejection is part of life. If one person rejects you, the next one may not. If other people reject you, that's *their* problem, not yours.

By admitting your hindrances and by taking these steps of action, you will be on your way to building exciting, fulfilling and rewarding relationships with others.

Say these things out loud right now: "I admit to the hindrances in my relationships."

"I have decided to overcome them."

"I am taking positive action to build positive relationships."

FIVE KEYS FOR STRONG RELATIONSHIPS

I want to give you five final keys that will help you excel as a person whom others want to be around.

The first relationship key is *communication.* Do you share yourself openly and freely? Do you share your thoughts and feelings? What excites you, and what brings you down? Do you share your good days and bad days? When people challenge or confront you, do you just become quiet? Are you an open, free, expressive, outgoing person? Or are you quiet, withdrawn and don't say much, even when people ask?

What is the condition of your ability to communicate? On a scale of 1 to 10, rate yourself with 1 being weak and 10 being strong.

The second key to building good relationships is *honesty.* Are you an honest person? Do you tell people when you're having a bad day? Do you share when you're feeling down? Do you let them know when you have failed? Are you honest about the negative things of your life as well as the positive? Do you hide, cover, excuse and rationalize your actions? Or do you tell the truth? Remember that to lie by omission is also a sin.

Give yourself a 1 to 10 rating in the area of honesty in relationships.

The third relationship key is *encouragement.* This is so important in relationships. People want and need to be encouraged. Do you try to lift others? Do you try to make people feel good and happy when they are around you? Are you a "lift" in the office or a "wet blanket"? Are you spreading joy and happiness or doom and gloom?

Give yourself a 1 to 10 rating as an encourager of people.

Relationship key number four is *giving*. Giving is a huge part in building strong relationships. Do you always want things your way? Or are you willing to give? In simple things like going to a restaurant for lunch, is it always your choice? Or do you let others choose as well? At dinner with friends, do you get out your calculator and figure out how much each owes? Or do you just give what you can and maybe cover someone else's meal? Are you a giving, generous person? Do you worry about other people's taking advantage of you? Or are you willing to give?

Rate yourself from 1 to 10 in the area of giving.

Finally, relationship key number five is *listening*. Do you really know those around you? Do you ask questions about their lives, their feelings, thoughts and ideas? Do you listen? If we could compare your jaw muscles to your ear muscles, which muscles would be in the best shape from the most activity? There is a saying that goes, "I have one mouth and two ears, so I'll listen twice as much as I talk."

How would you rate yourself in *really* listening and caring about people? I want to help with this 1 to 10 rating. Give yourself a 10 if you are interested in others and are careful to listen. Give yourself a 1 if you talk all the time and don't care about what they have to say.

Now take these five keys and examine the areas where your rating was low. Every one of us can improve in each of these areas. In the areas where you were weak, begin working to bring that rating up. For example, if you gave yourself a low rating in giving, begin to give without worrying about being paid back. If your score in encouraging wasn't very strong, write down some things you can say to uplift and encourage others. As you follow through on some of these things, you will begin to see a change in your relationships.

Building personal relationships is really a process of sowing and reaping. Every word you say is a seed; so is every gesture of kindness. In fact, everything you do with and for the people around you is a seed.

And that seed is going to grow up and produce good or bad fruit. So I encourage you to begin sowing good seed in others. Give yourself to others, and you will be enriched by new and improved relationships.

Finally, I invite you to say the following words out loud, over and over, until you believe them:

"I care about the people around me."

"I am willing to share myself intimately."

"I love others as I love myself."

Good relationships don't just happen. The way you treat others determines whether they will work with you or against you. This is the golden rule: **"Therefore, whatever you want men to do to you, you also do to them, for this is the Law and the Prophets** (Matt. 7:12).

Now that we've finished this practical section of mind renewal, we are ready to move on to the goal and main reason of mind renewal: to think like God thinks and do what He would do in the earth.

KEYS TO PERSONAL APPLICATION

"Personal relationships are a key to the success of your life."

1. How would you describe your relationships with the people you work with?

   _____

2. Has trying to change your spouse or some other close friend ever caused more problems in the relationship?

   _____

3. Of the five hindrances to intimacy, which one has been the biggest problem for you?

   _____

24

It's time to discover your fullest potential as a developing child of God. And I want to start this exposition on God's way of thinking with a part of an article I read some time ago. I think it will help you to conceive of the new you that God has always wanted you to be. And I'm also going to give you a little test; see if you can name the Bible character the article describes:

"He suffers from chronic, low-level depression. He's moody, impulsive and becomes angry when he feels victimized. He struggles with low self-worth. Because of feeling intellectually inferior, he attempts to hide behind an exaggerated ego. He really trusts no one. And yet he relies on others more than necessary and becomes naive in his relationships with them. He exhibits self-criticism and irritability.

"He believes in individualism, and has trouble with interpersonal relationships. His lack of trust often leaves him feeling anxious around people. He has relative weaknesses in attention, short-term working memory, verbal learning and fine motor coordination. He has trouble sleeping. His weight fluctuates. He's not mentally ill; he doesn't have a personality disorder, and yet he often feels humiliated, embarrassed and remorseful."

Did you guess who this could be? Well, first of all, outside of the Bible he or she could be anyone you might meet in your office tomorrow or any man or woman who wasn't raised with a biblical self-image—including you. But the Bible character this best describes is a young man by the name of Gideon. Let's look at him one more time, because Gideon is just like anyone. But God talked to him.

And if Gideon could believe what God said about him and get a new self-image, so can you.

When the Midianites were oppressing Gideon's land, his family was dealing with their own brand of super-high taxes and inflation. All around him was economic, cultural, religious and racial bondage. It was the worst of times for Israel. And Gideon was just flowing with it. He was just trying to survive. He wasn't thinking about being an overcomer or a prosperous individual.

When God called this young man of nineteen or twenty, he was hiding in the winepress, trying to thresh out some wheat. Threshing wheat in a winepress was a lousy, miserable, terrible way to do it. The chaff, the dust—everything—was miserable. The best way to thresh wheat in Gideon's day was on the threshing floor, where the wind would blow away the chaff, leaving only the kernels. But in the world, jobs are hard. The boss is difficult. The environment is bad. The freeway is a bummer. The bus is worse. I mean, no wonder some people have got to have a drink at lunch just to make it through another day!

But that day in the life of Gideon, the Angel of the Lord appeared to him, and his life was changed forever. He said, **"The Lord is with you, you mighty man of valor!"** (Judg. 6:12).

God told Gideon who he was, and the rest was up to him. This is how God talks to anyone who may be living below their potential. God doesn't say, "Here's your winning lottery ticket," or "Here's someone who will take care of your every need," or "Come on, it's time to escape—here's the Rapture."

No, God says, "You are a mighty man, a mighty woman of valor. Now come on, we have work to do."

When you take time to study what a *man of valor* is in your Hebrew dictionary, you will find that God called Gideon a champion-overcoming warrior who possessed valor, dignity and honor.

God told this insecure young man, "You're not what you think you are. Listen, you're what I say you are."

But the young man answered, "Look, uh, Lord, would You please look around? Look at me. Come on, I've been cooking french fries at McDonald's for eighteen years. I've been making minimum wage. I've just been trying to survive. I've just been trying to make it through life. Please, I don't need any problems. Look at my family; they're problem enough. I come from a family of dysfunctional people. We're all just surviving. So are my friends. We're all just trying to make a living. We're all crazy. Everybody I know is sick, divorced and in debt."

But God said, "All that's going to change, son. You are a mighty man of valor. As I am, so are you in this world." And this insecure, fearful young man from the tribe of Benjamin changed the course of his nation. Gideon went to war, and God fought with him:

> **Thus Midian was subdued before the children of Israel, so
> that they lifted their heads no more. And the country was quiet
> for forty years in the days of Gideon.**
>
> **Judges 8:28**

Are you still "seeing," as Gideon did, just enough to maintain and survive? Or are you now seeing that new business, that new ministry, that new relationship, that new strength, that new prosperity, that new peace and that new joy? Remember, the apostle Paul tells us in 1 John 4:17: **As He is, so are we in this world.** But you must see it first, because what you can see, you can be.

CHECK YOURSELF OUT

To help you see a little better, some of you need to go down to the best men's or women's store that you know of this week, put on the nicest suit or dress they have and check yourself. You need to step over in front of the mirror and say, "Umm-umm, yes. Now what shoes would you recommend for this particular style of suit? Maybe I could slip those on. Uh-huh. I need to see it in the natural light." Then you need to go out in front of the store and look again at your reflection in the display window.

Why?

To check out your new image.

Then you need to take that suit off and say, "I'll be back to purchase this another day."

After that you need to go down to the nicest car lot in town. Ask them to show you the best model on the lot. Pick out the color you like and sit in it. Smell it—there's nothing like the smell of a new car. Your car may smell old and burned out because of the catalytic converter that blew up two weeks ago. Every time you get in you get a whiff of that sulfur. You have to kick the cans out of the way to find your clutch. You stopped vacuuming it a year ago because the last time you did, it killed the vacuum. So you need to slide into that sparkling new model and just *see* yourself in it. *Remember, if you can see it, you can be it.* See yourself and say, "This is normal. This is me. This is who I am."

Now I know I'm only talking about silly material things. But if you can't see a new you in that realm, you'll never see it in the spiritual realm. You'll never see a new attitude. You'll never see a new vision for your future. You've got to see the new you and get a new vision before your eyes.

Some of you have always seen yourself as a T-shirt-and-jeans wearing, pot-bellied, hanging-in-there survivalist. Before you started reading this book, you saw yourself in a lounge chair, plopped down in front of a television set and simply trying to pay your bills and make it to the weekend.

You didn't see yourself succeeding.

You didn't see yourself overcoming or changing. You used to be excited when you could simply change your socks. But now your time has come to start seeing a new you.

You were made in the likeness and image of God, so it's time to start thinking like Him. By now you know what your real priorities are, and you know what God expects from you.

Do you suppose God walks into meetings thinking, *I sure hope this thing works out*? No, I think God goes into every meeting knowing exactly how it's going to work out. Do you think if God ever went to sleep, that He would wake up thinking, *Oh, I just hope I don't have another day like yesterday*? No, if He slept, I think He would be getting up every morning saying, "I'm new today. I'll go out and take dominion. All things are under My feet."

Do you see God as an excellent God? If you were to open God's sock drawer, do you think you would see forty-seven pairs of piled-up, unmatched socks? If you walked into God's house, do you think you would see stacks of newspapers all around? Would you have to make your way through Pepsi bottles and Coke cans all over the coffee table? Do you think He wouldn't be able to park His chariot in the garage because of garbage all piled up and tools hanging off the walls? Do you think His throne room is dusty and dirty, with piles of magazines strewn all over the place? No, you probably don't. But now, you—you're a different story, aren't you?

What does your house look like? What does your world look like? Now, I know this is a funny little analogy, but if you can't even organize your socks and underwear, it's no wonder you can't get yourself renewed, refreshed and going on in to your destiny.

If you can't even work it out to get your car in the garage, it's no wonder you can't get your life in gear. If your brain is so confused that your world is out of control, then you're not operating like God.

When I see God's throne, I see the headquarters of His glorious Church. I see glory and honor. I see accuracy. I see discipline. I see beauty. I see organization: Every planet is where it's supposed to be.

Every angel is doing what he's supposed to do. The choir is showing up on time. (Okay, I know they never leave.) Everything God does is done in excellence. So I work to fashion my home and church life as an embassy of God's throne.

Are you with me? You are God's family in the earth. You are created in His image and have been given His resources to reign on earth.

IT'S TIME TO GROW INTO YOUR NEW NAME

When you understand God's image inside of you, you understand that excellent is *your* name. You inherited it when He recreated your spirit. We touched on this a little in a previous chapter, but now I want to really bring it home.

O Lord, our Lord, how excellent is Your name in all the earth, You who set Your glory above the heavens!

Psalm 8:1

A name signifies much about the person it identifies. In the Old Testament, your name was changed if your character and position changed. Abram's name, "high father," was changed to Abraham, "father of a multitude," because of his courageous faith. Sarai's name, "princess," was changed to Sarah, "noblewoman," because of her courageous faith.

We see the same truth in the Gospels when Jesus changed Simon the fisherman's name from "swaying reed," to "rock," Peter. The Pharisee Saul's name was changed to Paul. And, looking again at Gideon, this young man's father changed his name from Gideon, "hewer; tree feller; warrior," to Jerubbaal, "Baal will contend," after he courageously tore down his father's pagan idol.

So your name describes your character and your being.

Every one of the Lord God's covenant names in the Old Testament pointed to one of His attributes. *Jehovah Tskidkenu* identifies God as

"Lord our righteousness." *Jehovah Rapha* reveals Him as "Lord our Healer." *Jehovah Jireh* means "Lord our Provider." *Jehovah Nissi* is "Lord our victory." *Jehovah Shammah* is "Lord our Shepherd," and so on. Look up the word *Lord* in your Hebrew dictionary and find how many times God's name describes His righteous being.

So when Psalm 8 says His name is excellent, that means everything about Him is excellent, including you, because He recreated you. As the most important piece in His art collection, you are His most important work! When anyone looks at the art of His creation, they must say, "Excellent!" When they look at the worlds and how accurate and well-balanced they are, they must exclaim, "Excellent!" And when they look at His renewed, well-balanced people, they must say, "Excellent!"—because God is excellent!

For example, if our planet were one degree off its axis, everything would change, and many on earth would die. If earth's annual orbit around the sun changed just a few miles, we would either burn or freeze. God is so accurate and so precise because He is excellent. Everything God put into the earth—from the growth of a seed to the intricacies of mathematics—is excellent, because God is excellent.

Now look at how you and I are mentioned in Psalm 8, verses 3 and 4: **When I consider Your heavens, the work of Your fingers, the moon and the stars, which You have ordained, what is man that You are mindful of him, and the son of man that You visit him?**

In these verses David says, "Why in the world would You want to visit with us, excellent Lord? Why are we so important to You? When we look at the glory of the universe and realize that You want to be involved with us, wow!" **For You have made [us] a little lower than the angels, and You have crowned [us] with glory and honor** (v. 5). The *King James* translates the Hebrew word for *God* in this passage, as "angels." But the Hebrew actually says "Elohim."[1] It is the same word that describes God the Creator in Genesis 1:1, **In the beginning God**

[Elohim] **created the heavens and the earth.** And man has been made just a little lower than Him!

Mankind isn't lower than angels because Paul says in 1 Corinthians 6:3 that we Christians will judge angels. Hebrews 1:14 says angels are sent to be servants of the heirs of salvation. And we are those heirs! We're just a little lower than God. What an image this produces in my spirit! And it should do the same for you.

All right, hold on to your seat now, because we're not done yet. Psalm 8:5 says, **You have crowned [us] with glory and honor.** The angry preacher would say, "He crowned us with a club!" But the truth says, "He crowned man with glory and honor." The angry preacher says, "He crowned us with sickness and poverty." But the truth says, "He crowned us with glory and honor." Religion says, "He clubbed us to humble us." God says, "He crowned us to exalt us in glory and honor."

If God says this about man, then that ought to settle it.

In verses 6-8 of this powerful Psalm, your God-given image looks even better:

> **You have made him to have dominion over the works of Your hands; You have put all things under his feet, all sheep and oxen—even the beasts of the field, the birds of the air, and the fish of the sea that pass through the paths of the seas.**

These verses remind you of your dominion. Then in verse 9 the psalmist writes again: **O Lord, our Lord, how excellent is Your name in all the earth!**

Notice how this chapter doesn't say, "You're going to get dominion when you go to heaven." No, it says, "You've been made to have dominion."

It doesn't say, "All things are going to be under your feet in the Rapture." No, it says, "He's already put all things under your feet."

You know, I used to have size 13 shoes. But in the last few years, the Lord has told me to expand my ministry. So my feet have grown to size 15. I think it's so I can get more things under my feet! (Okay, well they feel like they've grown anyway.) I've been crowned with glory and honor. I've been given dominion. (I went to Dominion College!) And all things are under my feet.

When you understand excellence, you understand that you aren't under the circumstances of life; they are under you! All things are under your feet. Once you can begin to *see* it, you can begin to *be* it.

Proverbs 22:9 (AMP) says, **A bountiful eye shall be blessed.** Or, "If you can see it, you can have it." So God told Abram, "Lift up your eyes and look north, south, east and west. All the land that you see I've given to you and your descendants. If you can see it, Abram, you can have it. If you can see it, you can be it."

God told Joshua, "Go ahead, Josh, look and see that I have given you Jericho!" The walls were shut up. It wasn't in their hands at that time. But if Joshua could see it, he could have it.

When you can see as God sees, it will take the fear out of life. It takes the laziness out. It takes the negative attitudes out. You get up every morning, crowned with glory and honor. You face every day, knowing you have dominion. You walk into every circumstance, knowing it's under your feet! That's the way God wants you to live! Why? Because you were made in *His* likeness and in *His* image!

How Excellent Is Your Name, Believer!

How excellent is *your* name, believer! That means everything you do should emanate God's excellence. The *King James Version* of Proverbs 12:26 says, **The righteous is more excellent than his neighbour.**

So when someone drives by your house, they should say, "Oh, Christians—they're the most excellent folks in our neighborhood."

When they see your kids, they should say, "They must be Christians." When they see you on the job, they should say, "Oh, there's a Christian. You can just tell—he's more excellent than anybody else at work." If they snuck into your closet, they should be able to say, "Oh, yep, Christian—neat, clean, anointed."

Now, I'm using these purely natural things simply to challenge your thinking. God is excellent and has chosen to bless all who receive Him with that excellence. It comes with our new family name. So we should be reflecting Him daily as we are transformed from glory to glory into His glorious Church—because we are blessed!

YOU ARE BLESSED!

Blessed be the God and Father of our Lord Jesus Christ, who has blessed us with every spiritual blessing in the heavenly places in Christ.

Ephesians 1:3

Paul is telling us here that God has already blessed you with everything heaven has to offer. So stop right here for a second and say, "I'm already blessed!" So many Christians are trying to get God to do something, without knowing He has already done it. That's right—God has already provided whatever you need. Right now, you're blessed with everything heaven has to offer. And if you can see this image of total blessing, it will change the way you live.

How you see God is how you see your world. If your image of God sounds like, "Well, God might heal, but you never know," "God might bless, but you can never be sure," "God touches some, but He doesn't touch others," or "God prospers some, but others, He wants to be poor," then these images will become the controlling factor in your life and you will act that way. Sometimes you will be generous; sometimes you will be stingy. You might be nice to some and unkind to others, because your image of God is your image of yourself.

But once you see in Ephesians 1:3 that God has *already* blessed you with everything heaven has to offer, it is *easy* to receive from heaven. It is also easy to give, because understanding that every spiritual blessing in the heavens is yours leaves very little limitation on what you have.

When your mind is renewed in the revelation that you are blessed, you will just flow. You won't be selfish or guarded. You won't be defensive. You will be a big, open, generous, liberal person. Because God is big, you will see big.

Paul continues to tell us of our special position in Christ in Ephesians 2:5-10:

> **Even when we were dead in trespasses, [God has] made us alive together with Christ (by grace you have been saved), and has raised us up together, and made us sit together in the heavenly places in Christ Jesus, that in the ages to come He might show the exceeding riches of His grace in His kindness toward us in Christ Jesus. For by grace you have been saved through faith, and that not of yourselves; it is the gift of God, not of works, lest anyone should boast. For we are His workmanship, created in Christ Jesus for good works, which God prepared beforehand that we should walk in them.**

Even when you were dead in trespasses, Paul writes, "God made you alive with Christ. Then He raised you up and made you to sit in His heavenly places in Christ Jesus." Wow!

So many folks are trying to get Jesus to come down to their problems, into their negativity, and they have no idea that they have already been raised up! God wants us to live up to His presence because we are seated in Christ at His right hand.

This is your image! This is the way a believer who is grounded in God's truth should think!

But the last place Satan wants you to see yourself is seated in the heavens with Christ. Why? Because when you're seated in heavenly places it's not hard to resist temptation, and that puts him out of business.

You see, if you're just a no-good sinner, you might as well go ahead and get drunk, have a foolish affair and be stupid. But if you're seated in heavenly places in Christ, you won't live that way, because Jesus doesn't live that way. You will also understand that your new image is an eternal image, because in verse 7 Paul writes, **That in the ages to come He might show the exceeding riches of His grace in His kindness toward us in Christ Jesus.** Now, if that doesn't thrill your soul, I don't know what will.

Check Us Out!

In the ages to come, God wants to show the universe how kind He is by how He treats you and me. This may happen next month, in a thousand years or even in fifty million years. But it will happen. We'll be living honestly, with integrity, love and big, open hearts. We'll be moving in Him, crowned with glory and honor, blessed with everything heaven has to offer. And God will say, "Those are My kids. Check them out." And the whole universe will see His kindness.

I don't know who in the universe will be looking. Maybe the devil. Maybe God's angels. I don't know who's going to be checking us out. But they're going to say, "God is kind. God is good. O Lord, how excellent is Your name."

Similarly, when those of us in the Church see your kids, we learn about you. I love to watch kids pour into our elementary school at Christian Faith Center. Their uniforms are clean, and they've got them on straight. Their ties are straight. They're awake, and they've had breakfast. And when I see this, I think, *Those parents have it together. They have a happy, disciplined home. What good parents!*

When I see some kids going to public schools, they're dragging their books. Their pants are wrinkled and sagging. Their shirts are hanging out. Their hair is semi-combed. And when you see them, you hurt and have to say, "Those poor children are either homeless or their parents are lousy."

The same kind of thinking happens when the world looks at the Church. When the world looks at you, they see God through your image. They see your spirit, attitude, generosity, forgiveness, quickness to serve and your love. And they say, "Oh, you've got a great God."

When the world comes to your home, they should be able to look around and see the goodness of God. I'm not talking about possessions. I'm talking about the image of God that is reflected in your home. They should sense His Spirit and attitude. The material part is just a small manifestation. But when they look at us, they should say, "I want to go to your church. I want to find out more about your God."

Non-Christians look at the Church world in general today and don't break down our doors to get in church. Why? We're not the glorious Church Jesus died to give birth to. So we've got to get to the place where we've been transformed into *His* image. And because you're involved in the process, you are on the way. When the world looks at you, you should be a shining representation of Jesus Christ on the earth. And this should inspire them to say, "How can I get to your God?" "Come on, it's not hard," we should be able to tell them, "You're going to have fun. You're going to love it." Isn't that a whole lot better than telling them, "turn or burn"? Isn't that a whole lot better than, "God is gonna get you!"

Remember, 1 John 4:17 says, **As He is, so are we in this world—** right here and now, in the face of the devil, when it's easy to be mad, when it's normal to be sad, when it's easy to get upset, and all the negative stuff that comes so naturally is swirling around us. But as He is, so are we *in this world*. Not when we get to heaven. Not on the other side. Not after the Rapture. Now.

And He is graceful, forgiving, loving, disciplined, energized, excited, motivated, overcoming, healing and always providing. Jesus has an answer for every problem. He has grace for every circumstance. He has power for every situation. And He wants to help others through you.

When you let God's thoughts become your thoughts and His ways your ways, you will be amazed at what you can do. And people will want to join you. People don't want religion. They don't want some mean, ugly preacher looking down on them, pointing a bony, judgmental finger while they hear some hardball sermon. But they do want to hear about how they can have a brighter and more beautiful life. And when they see you living it, they will ask.

Let's move on to our last chapter now, you mighty men and women of valor, for seven final steps to a glorious new you!

25

Now I want to share from my heart some of the nitty-gritty details involved in changing your life.

The choices we make every day affect where we will be the next day. And there are always people, places and situations the enemy will use to lure you off God's path. So I want to get very practical in this chapter. I have seven final steps that will help you break the carnal attitudes and habits that keep you from God's best in life.

STEP 1: KNOW THE NEW YOU

So who do you think you are? Who are you trying to be today? Are you still just trying to survive, hiding out from the "Midianites" in your own little corner? Or are you ready to stand up and receive your calling?

The new you, you mighty Christian of valor, is just like Jesus. This is the new you. The Bible says you're a Christian—Christlike—and that you should want to live like He lived. When problems arise, you can solve them. Like Jesus, you can overcome them. When people have needs, you meet them. You have answers and solutions, and you live above circumstances. This is who you are.

When situations come up that aren't always good, you, Christian, always win. You overcome. I mean if five thousand people show up for lunch, you find a way to feed them. When the neighbor's daughter is dying, you help them get her healed. If your friends are confused and sad, you have an answer that brings joy and peace. Because you know the new you, you share Christ's vision and have His discipline to fulfill it. As He is, so are you in this world. So step 1 is knowing the new you.

STEP 2: MEDITATE ON THE NEW YOU

Step 2 has to do with allowing God to change you into that new Christian image through mediating on the transforming truths of His Word. Philippians 4:8 says we are to think on these truths: Whatever is true, honest, just, pure, lovely, of good report, virtuous and praiseworthy, think on these things. Think about these things, Paul instructs us. *The Amplified Bible* says to fix your mind on the things the Bible says about the new you.

When you drive to work in the morning, don't fix your mind on what's gone wrong and what you're afraid could happen.

Not long ago, we were on our way to the airport. I can't remember who was driving, but we pulled over to get into the car pool lane. Well, this driver started honking, and I started laughing. I looked at Wendy and said, "It's not even 6 AM and this guy's mad." Why? Because we got in *his* lane. Now, I know I should have known this man *owned* that lane, but live and learn.

Anyway, I mentioned to our driver how sad it was that this man was on his way to another miserable day and He was upset before he even got to work. His heart rate may have been throbbing through his brain. That night he would wonder why he was so tired, why the day was so sad and why all his work associates can't stand him. The reason? His image. The image this man had of himself and his world was no doubt very negative. And the same can happen to a Christian if he doesn't meditate on the new person he's become.

When you're meditating on what God's Word has to say about you, you don't get up thinking about your sickness. You get up seeing yourself healthy and whole. You don't get out of bed thinking about your bills. You get out of bed thinking about how God meets all your needs according to His riches in glory. When you're mediating on the Word, you don't turn on the television to find out who died, the latest disaster or who's been having sex with the wrong person—before 6 AM. No, you just open your Bible, find something good about your God and yourself and fix your mind on it. You meditate on the new you.

Psalm 1:1 says, **Blessed is the man who walks not in the counsel of the ungodly, nor stands in the path of sinners, nor sits in the seat of the scornful.**

If you walk with the ungodly, pretty soon you're going to be standing and sitting with them. So don't do that.

Verses 2-3 show us the "new you" way:

> **But his delight is in the law of the Lord, and in His law he meditates day and night. He shall be like a tree planted by the rivers of water, that brings forth its fruit in its season, whose leaf also shall not wither; and whatever he does shall prosper.**

This is what the new you needs to mediate on: on God and His promises. Meditate on how Jesus walked, because that's how you are to walk.

The Joshua 1:8 meditation promise is yours every day, because that's what the new you wants to do:

> **"This Book of the Law shall not depart from your mouth, but you shall meditate in it day and night, that you may observe to do according to all that is written in it. For then you will make your way prosperous, and then you will have good success."**

When you meditate on God's Word, you prosper and have good success. You raise your level of prosperity just by what you focus on. But you will never do it if you choose to think like your local union, your corporate bosses or the ungodly world media.

"Well, Brother Treat, I can't get my boss to give me a raise!" So! Since when does your boss control your life? If your mind is on God and you're doing what He wants you to do, He will either change your boss or move your boss. It shouldn't matter what your boss does.

"But the government said..." Well, see, the government isn't in control of your destiny.

When you meditate on what God says, He will be the controlling factor of your life. Colossians 3:16-17 says:

> Let the word of Christ dwell in you richly in all wisdom, teaching and admonishing one another in psalms, hymns, and spiritual songs, singing with grace in your hearts to the Lord. And whatever you do in word or deed, do all in the name of the Lord Jesus, giving thanks to God the Father through Him.

Another way to read this passage is, "When you let the Word of God dwell in you richly, whatever you do will be done in the name of the Lord. You will prosper and give the Father thanks."

So step 2 is meditating on the new you.

STEP 3: HANG OUT WITH THE NEW YOU

Step 3 is spending time with others who share your vision of godly change. In other words, hang out with the new you! Build relationships with people who are going where you want to go or are already *there*. If you get on a bus with a group of folks who are going to Tacoma and you want to go to Vancouver and you say, "These people are all my old friends. We've been together since high school. I mean, we've been through so much. We're so close!" Guess what? You won't make it to Vancouver!

Proverbs 13:20 says, **He who walks with wise men will be wise, but the companion of fools will be destroyed.** When strife came up between Abram's and Lot's men, for example, Abram told Lot to choose a direction, and *get!*

He said, **"Is not the whole land before you? Please separate from me. If you take the left, then I will go to the right; or, if you go to the right, then I will go to the left"** (Gen. 13:9).

Lot, by the way, means *"veil."*[1] And to use him as a parallel, most people have a veiled or hidden, selfish agenda. As long as Lot was hanging around Abram, God was limited in what He could do. So Lot moved on and pitched his tent towards Sodom. And the moment Lot left, God showed up and furthered Abram's vision. Lot couldn't keep his herdsmen under control, and the strife of it all confused Abram's journey. So Abram had to get his social relationships right before God would lead him any further spiritually.

"Yeah, but they're my friends," you say. All right, so you'll have to either give up your destiny and destination in Christ, or you'll have to give up those relationships. Which one is it going to be? "Well, can't I do both?" Sure, just start fulfilling your call to share the gospel in their lives, and they'll either get saved or separate. Otherwise you will get caught up in what they call the "paralysis of analysis." You will develop into what the Bible calls an unstable, double-minded person (James 1:8) because you refuse to make right choices.

A double-minded Christian will say: "I don't want to leave my old friends, but I do want to go to a new destination. I don't want to give up the world, but I sure wish I could make heaven. I don't want to give up my Haagen-Dazs, but I would like to lose five pounds."

Well, you have a situation here, and it's not going to come out well if you don't learn to make important choices. You have to make the right choice by hanging out with the new you.

When I met the Lord at nineteen, all the people I knew were losers spelled with capital letters: LOSERS! All the friends I'd been hanging out with were just like I used to be, because they'd hung around me!

Four of my old friends even came into the rehab program with me. One of them was a girl I knew in high school. Three of them were guys I had run around with. They all came in saying, "Oh, yeah, man, we want this. Oh, yeah, man."

But I knew they weren't sincere, and when they tried to get me to compromise and leave with them, I told them to hit the road. "Come on, man! We're friends, we're family, we're blood brothers, man! Let's go!"

I had to make a choice, so I said, "This is where I'm going. As long as you want to go with me, we're brothers. But if you don't want to go with me, that's your choice." I haven't seen any of my old druggie friends for twenty some years now. But one of them called me a few years ago from the penitentiary.

All the old clichés are full of truth: Birds of a feather flock together. If you sleep with the dogs, you'll get fleas. If you hang out with chickens, you'll only stir up a little dirt in life and eat dirty things.

God isn't going to show you the future if you're hanging out with people who can sabotage your future. So you have to decide, "Am I going to keep hanging with the chickens? Or am I going to fly with the eagles? Am I going to be a fryer or a flyer?" It's always your choice.

What's more important to you, accommodating the past? Or moving toward the future? Pleasing God or pleasing all the losers in your world?

Jesus said, **"Do not think that I came to bring peace on earth. I did not come to bring peace but a sword"** (Matt. 10:34). Now this is Jesus talking, and remember, He is the Prince of Peace. Basically, what He said was, "Now look, guys, I didn't come to compromise and make everything nice and smooth. I've come with a sword, because in some situations you're going to have to cut some stuff off."

Man, I love this verse because Jesus is saying, "You've got to decide who you're going to hang out with."

Someone might say, "Well, I just don't think y'all should be going to that church over there with all of that Bible preaching and praying in tongues. I think that's a cult."

"Oh, you do? Really? You think Jesus Christ came to lead a cult?" Now, if your father or mother says something like that, this is a tough one. Maybe your best friend before you were saved would say it.

But you have to make a choice. Are you going to follow someone who is on the wrong bus to nowhere? When your ministry call is sending you to Vancouver and your friends and family are going to Tacoma to serve themselves, where will you go? I don't mean you aren't to love them and lead them to Jesus. Of course you are to do that. But they will never help you prosper until they know God. They will never help your marriage be any better. They will never help you fulfill your destiny and the will of God in your life.

The reason I'm spending so much time on this step is because I see so many people who let relationships with people who are going nowhere keep them from going somewhere, and it upsets me. They hang out with their "real nowhere man," and they let that old, flaky relationship keep them from their destiny.

You must make the choice: eagle or chicken, flyer or fryer. So get rid of those damaging, ungodly relationships! Be a glorious light to everyone you know, but don't let everyone put your light out.

STEP 4: ACT LIKE THE NEW YOU

Step 4 in the transformation process is to start acting like the new you. And you can start acting different once you start meditating on God's biblical truths.

For if anyone is a hearer of the word and not a doer, he is like a man observing his natural face in a mirror; for he observes himself, goes away, and immediately forgets what kind of man he was. But he who looks into the perfect law of liberty and

continues in it, and is not a forgetful hearer but a doer of the work, this one will be blessed in what he does.

James 1:23-25

In this passage James says the believer is blessed by his deeds, not by his good intentions. If all you do is *plan* to act, the blessing never comes.

Listen, you have to act differently before you feel differently. You have to get up and go when you don't want to go at times, and it's always uncomfortable. But this is so important, because when choose to *act* like the new you, when you start doing the things God's Word says to do, He will back you up.

Now here's where people get hung up because they start feeling like, *Well, this isn't natural. This doesn't feel normal.* And that's true enough. If you've felt like a loser your whole life, it's very abnormal to act like a winner.

When I went to a coach to work on my golf swing, he said, "What is that?"

I thought I had it together.

So I said, "That's my swing. I'm pretty cool, aren't I?"

"No, not really," he said, "you're all messed up."

So I had to reposition. I had some changing to do. I felt comfortable with my old swing, but I wanted to change. And as I practiced over and over, his new and improved power swing slowly became mine.

You want to talk about unnatural? The first year of my Christian life was very unnatural for me. I couldn't imagine living a life in which I never smoked a cigarette, never smoked a joint, never drank a beer and never drank a cocktail. But I stayed with it and chose to act like a Christian, regardless of how uncomfortable I felt at times.

I remember the first time I lifted my hands in church. I was very uncomfortable, thinking *I'm just acting like one of these guys.* I'd listen to what the person sitting next to me would say: "Praise the Lord! Amen, hallelujah! I love You, Jesus, I love You...I really do love You, Jesus," and I would say it too. I didn't know I was doing what the Scripture said to do: "Lift up holy hands and praise the Lord." I was acting—you could even say faking it—but I wasn't doing it out of some phony hidden agenda. I just didn't know what to do, so I acted like those around me who did.

After a few months in church, the real me was "square." The real me liked to lift up hands. The real me liked to pray. The real me enjoyed being "straight." And the old me was gone! I had been transformed into His image in that area of my life.

Some people aren't used to looking people in the eye and smiling. They're more used to slipping into church after the service has started. They're used to showing up late everywhere. Their life is late. They were born late. When we all get to heaven, they'll be late! We'll have to give them a video of the first three days of the seven days of the Lord's Supper!

No one who has sat on the bench most of their life is used to going out on the field and saying, "Give me the ball, coach! I know I can do it. We are the winners! We are the champions!" They're not used to having money after they pay all the bills with their paycheck. They're used to having too much month at the end of their money! But if they would only start acting on the truths of Scripture, even if it feels abnormal, they could move to a higher level. And eventually they would begin to act like Jesus.

Everything that feels normal in life has you where you are today. So if you want to develop new and better habits, you must be willing to do some things that feel very abnormal. When I would tell the golf coach, "Well, that doesn't feel right," he would say, "That's okay. Keep trying it, and eventually it will feel comfortable."

If you keep doing what feels normal, you will only get more of what you have! But once you decide to start saying words you've never said before, thinking thoughts you've never had before and hanging out with people you never hung out with before, you will change.

But you are the one who must choose to get up and move out of that place you have been living in life. If you want to make more money, have more influence and win people to Jesus, you will have to make it a daily habit to stop acting like the old you. And once you know the new you, start hanging out with and meditating on the new you—the fourth step—acting like the new you, won't be that hard.

When you get around new people you will act like a new person yourself, and you will start living on another level. Jesus said:

> **"Therefore whoever hears these sayings of Mine, and does them, I will liken him to a wise man who built his house on the rock: and the rain descended, the floods came, and the winds blew and beat on that house; and it did not fall, for it was founded on the rock."**

> **Matthew 7:24-25**

James 1:24-25 says that the doer of God's Word is blessed. The hearers only stay deluded.

STEP 5: TALK LIKE THE NEW YOU

Step 5 in the transformational process is talking like the new you.

You can't talk the same way you used to talk before you came to Christ. You can't walk around saying, "Well, I can't afford it, I don't have time, I'm so tired, my back hurts so bad; it's killing me. If my back doesn't kill me, this migraine headache will bury me. And if that doesn't do me in, my asthma, bursitis or ulcer will get me."

Why can't you talk like that? Because Proverbs 18:21 says, **Death and life are in the power of the tongue.** When God declares a thing, it frames the universe around Him, and God wants His children to talk like He talks.

Romans 4:17 says that God calls things that are not, as though they were. When God looked out over the universe in Genesis 1, He didn't say, "Woo! It's dark out there! Man, it's really dark!" No. God said, **"Let there be light,"** and light was. God looked at the darkness and spoke light into existence.

Isn't it interesting how in the first chapter of Genesis, over and over again it says, "God said and said and said." Hebrews 11:3 says, **By faith we understand that the worlds were framed by the word of God.** And because you are created in God's likeness and image, He wants your words to frame your world.

So if you say things like, "Well, we've just been in debt, I was born in debt, my parents were in debt, I was raised in debt; I can't afford that" and so forth, you just framed your world with debt upon debt. And as long as you keep talking that way about finances, you will live that way.

But if you act like God, you will speak light to the darkness. You will prophesy light to that big hole in your checkbook. You will raise that thing from the dead! Because God calls things that are not as though they were, and because you are made in His image, you can too!

So when you begin to say, "I'm financially prospering, I don't live in debt, I pay off my debts, my home is paid for, I have a car paid for, I have money in the bank, God gives me the power to get wealth, money is coming to me," you are only obeying what God's Word says and framing your life with God's supernatural best.

Remember, the old apostle wouldn't have prayed his 3 John 2 prayer, if he didn't mean it:

> Beloved, I pray that you may prosper in all things and be in health, just as your soul prospers.

And the context of 2 Corinthians 8:9 in reference to the generosity of the Macedonian church is finances:

> For I bear witness that according to their ability, yes, and beyond their ability, they were freely willing, imploring us with much urgency that we would receive the gift and the fellowship of the ministering to the saints.... For you know the grace of our Lord Jesus Christ, that though He was rich, yet for your sakes He became poor, that you through His poverty might become rich.

> 2 Corinthians 8:3,4,9

Now you may be thinking, *Wow, I could never say that.* And that's why you are where you are. That's why you don't experience all God has for you and why you don't have the influence on others God wants you to have.

What about your health? What if you always say things like, "My back is killing me. And my migraine, it seems to be worse today. Oh, and let me tell you about my asthma—man, is it acting up. It's October, and my asthma always acts up. In November, my bursitis and my arthritis start flaring up. It does every year. And you know, in December, I always get those winter colds." When you speak as if sickness is a normal part of your life, it will be.

If you look in the medicine cabinet of people who speak like that, you'll see that they look like a drugstore. Why? Because those people believe daily for sickness. They frame their world with sickness. They expect sickness, so they confess sickness. When they walk into their offices, they start framing their offices with their sickness: "Man, I had a tough week, and a headache knocked me out. Then my back went out." And someone else will get in on it. "I know what you're saying. I can relate to that. I got some of these new pills. You ever tried these?"

But if that same office worker knew the power of words, he would show up for work saying, "I just want you all to know I'm healed, from the top of my head to the soles of my feet. I just want you all to know I'm feeling good. I'm blessed. I think I'll just go ahead and live healthy for about 120 years." And as soon as those words came out of his mouth, the others in the office would grumble and say, "What in the world is wrong with you?" Why? Because it really ticks the devil's crowd off when you go framing your world with your words. Now isn't it sad that if you confess your pains, you're normal. But if you confess your health, you're weird.

When you're a new creation in Christ, you need to talk like the new you! You need to start talking words like: "He Himself bore my sins on the tree that I might die unto sin and live unto righteousness, for by His stripes I have been healed! (1 Peter 2:24.) I'm healed and I'm whole, in the name of Jesus. I can do all things through Christ who strengthens me! (Phil. 4:13.) With long life He satisfies me and lets me behold His salvation! (Ps. 91:16.) I have time to do everything I want to do and live like I want to live."

You need to talk God's promises to let the power of God's Word confirm His blessings in your life. You need to be speaking the blessing over your life and saying things like, "My marriage is healthy; my relationship is strong," instead of, "I don't understand what's going on with my wife. Who could understand women anyway? My God, it gives me a headache!" Because you were made in God's image, you've got to *guard* your tongue.

At first this transformation step may seem strange and uncomfortable. But be bold in your speech, frame your world with God's will and your words and He will back you up.

STEP 6: SEE THE NEW YOU

Step 6 in the transformational process is seeing the new you, the new you that's living from glory to glory and looks like Jesus, so that when you look in the mirror, you see the *new* you. Not the you who got divorced, went bankrupt or had been sick and poor. No, you need to see the new you who is being transformed into the image of Jesus and going from glory to glory.

This is really the hardest step for many believers. But remember, if you can see it, you can be it.

Proverbs 22:9 KJV says, **He who hath a bountiful eye shall be blessed.** What is a bountiful eye? It's the "good eye" Jesus spoke about in Matthew 6:22: **"The lamp of the body is the eye. If therefore your eye is good, your whole body will be full of light."**

The bountiful eye sees bountiful blessing and abundance. It sees opportunities abounding. The bountiful eye sees the glass half full, not half empty. There are customers and opportunities in abundance. There are new clients waiting for you to call. So what if you already called three people and they said no? A bountiful eye knows someone's going to say yes. It sees abundance.

But most important, the bountiful eye sees the new you. And you must see the new you to get up and out of your old living patterns. Remember, Jesus said in Matthew 6:22-23:

> **"If therefore your eye is good, your whole body will be full of light. But if your eye is bad, your whole body will be full of darkness. If therefore the light that is in you is darkness, how great is that darkness!"**

The difference between, for instance, a marriage succeeding and a marriage failing is the kind of *eyes* you have. A bountiful eye will be blessed and full of light. A negative eye will be dark and cursed. If you always see green on the other side of the fence, then it's not your side of the fence that's the problem—it's your eye.

When they were dating, some people only saw the beautiful side of their future mate. They only saw that beautiful smile and the other parts they liked because their eye was bountiful, hopeful, loving and full of light. But then, once they had been married a few years, they began looking for a way out. Why? Their eye that was once full of light turned to darkness, and all they could think of was what they didn't like.

When you look in the mirror, do you only see those places in your body that you wish were different? "Well, how come I'm so big here and so small there? I wish I could take some of that off here, and put it over there." How are your eyes?

JACOB'S SPECKLED FLOCKS

There is an interesting story in Genesis 30 that isn't very commonly taught. But it illustrates this truth so powerfully. It has to do with Jacob's bountiful eye that helped him finally break free from his father-in-law, Laban's bondage.

> **Now Jacob took for himself rods of green poplar and of the almond and chestnut trees, peeled white strips in them, and exposed the white which was in the rods. And the rods which he had peeled, he set before the flocks in the gutters, in the watering troughs where the flocks came to drink, so that they should conceive when they came to drink. So the flocks conceived before the rods, and the flocks brought forth streaked, speckled, and spotted.**
>
> **Genesis 30:37-39**

Now, this sounds odd, but let me go back and give you a little bit of background to explain what was happening. In this situation, Jacob had worked seven years for his perspective father-in-law, Laban, to marry his daughter Rachel. But after seven years, Laban gave Jacob his daughter, Leah, instead. He was told that he would have to work another seven years to marry Rachel.

So now, after fourteen years, Jacob was wanting to move on. He wanted to get on with his own life, his family and his business. But he had worked for Laban all these years and had nothing of his own. Jacob was like so many of us today—who, if they quit working today, they wouldn't have an income tomorrow.

Jacob had no wealth. He had no assets. He worked for "the man." And he had to keep working for the man, because if he missed a week, he couldn't pay his bills.

So Jacob came up with a plan. He went to Laban and said, "Look, the feeble sheep in your herd are the brown, the spotted and the speckled. They aren't pure white. They don't produce good wool. They're not strong animals. So could I have them? I've worked faithfully for you and caused your company to prosper, so could I have the feeble sheep? Then, whatever they breed on their own will be my little flock. And if the flock gets large enough, that will be my time to go. Okay?"

Well, you know, Laban must have thought, *this is good! This is going to be great because there's only a few brown sheep. And it isn't any big deal. So I'll keep this guy working for me for a long time. I know I've been blessed because of his presence, and this ought to keep it going for a good, long time.*

But Jacob received a word from the Lord. There is no other way to explain this, because what happened was miraculous. So Jacob took the poplar, almond and chestnut trees and peeled them. These trees were streaked and spotted. Then he placed these branches in the water troughs the sheep drink from. Verse 39 says, **The flocks conceived before the rods.** And when they were born, they were born streaked and speckled.

Do you think the rods caused the flocks to conceive streaked, speck-led and spotted lambs? Do you think a branch lying in the water could change the color of a sheep? No—that is, not unless God gives you a word. Only God can alter life in any way. So this story, in particular illustrates how what a person sees can decide what he can conceive in life when God is his source, and He wills a thing.

Remember, if you keep looking at what you have, all you will have is more of what you've already got! But if you start seeing something bigger and better, something holy, pure and godly in the image of Jesus, you will conceive that!

The bountiful eye sees that the end of a thing is much better than its beginning. (Eccl. 7:8.) Verses 40-43 of Genesis 30 finish the story:

> **Then Jacob separated the lambs, and made the flocks face toward the streaked and all the brown in the flock of Laban; but he put his own flocks by themselves and did not put them with Laban's flock.**

> **And it came to pass, whenever the stronger livestock conceived, that Jacob placed the rods before the eyes of the livestock in the gutters, that they might conceive among the rods.**

> **But when the flocks were feeble, he did not put them in; so the feebler were Laban's and the stronger Jacob's.**

> **Thus the man became exceedingly prosperous, and had large flocks, female and male servants, and camels and donkeys.**

Jacob received a vision and began to see himself in a new light. He had worked as a ranch hand fourteen years, but once he broke out of his minimum-wage mentality, his flocks became bigger than Laban's. And in the next chapter of Genesis, he took off on his own.

STEP 7: PRAY WITH THE SPIRIT OF THE NEW YOU

Finally, step number 7 in the transformational process is accepting God's invitation to pray with the spirit of the new you. The new man who is being renewed according to the image of Him who created him doesn't pray old, whining prayers like, "I'm so tired, Lord. God, don't You see what I'm going through?" No, the new man will pray in accordance with the spirit of the new you. That means praying in other tongues.

Why would Jesus tell His followers in one of His last most important messages on earth to pray with new tongues? Because He knew that if they didn't receive their new prayer language, they wouldn't enter a new level of life.

The Bible says that when you pray with an unknown tongue, your spirit prays with the Holy Spirit. Paul tells us in Romans 8:26-27 that when we don't know how to pray for a situation mentally, the Spirit will pray a perfect prayer of faith in His language to bring His will to pass.

Jude 20-21 says that you build up your most holy faith and stay in the love of God when you pray in the Spirit:

But you, beloved, building yourselves up on your most holy faith, praying in the Holy Spirit, keep yourselves in the love of God, looking for the mercy of our Lord Jesus Christ unto eternal life.

And Jesus said in Mark 16:17 that tongues would be one of the signs of a true believer: "**And these signs will follow those who believe: In My name they will cast out demons; they will speak with new tongues.**"

God invites every one of His new creations to pray with His new language. He didn't stop the whole deal at the death of the last apostle. He didn't favor just those twelve and leave the rest of history without this wonderful blessing.

When you only pray in English or some other natural human language out of your mind, you are praying at your own mental level.

But every time you choose to pray in the Spirit, you empower the new you to communicate with God beyond your mental abilities.

First Corinthians 14:2,4 says when you pray with the spirit, you speak mysteries and build yourself up in faith:

> **For he who speaks in a tongue does not speak to men but to God, for no one understands him; however, in the spirit he speaks mysteries.... He who speaks in a tongue edifies himself, but he who prophesies edifies the church.**

When you begin to pray in other tongues, there is unlimited communication. Your spirit is in tune and praying with God's Spirit, giving you access to His level. It's imperative to do so. It is so big.

Prayer in tongues is one of the most important parts of building the new you. Why do you suppose the enemy fights it so hard? Why do we argue the issue? Why do we avoid the subject so often? Because it is so big. It's so powerful. When you pray in the spirit you are constantly in touch with the spirit of the new you who was recreated in the glorious image of God. When you pray in tongues you supersede the old carnal you and the Holy Spirit keeps drawing you toward Himself. Tongues are His language. He draws you toward your destiny and the glory of God.

I believe one of the reasons Wendy and I came out of the poverty, barely-get-by, just-pay-your-bills-and-live-in-debt mentality of the world was that we caught this at a young age. I'm not sure how we did it. I'm not even sure we were taught. Sometimes it's caught, not just taught. But somehow we caught it. And we'd just pray in the Spirit all the time.

We'd pray in tongues while we were driving. We'd pray in tongues while we were working around the house. We'd pray in tongues while we were studying. Without our even knowing it back in those early days, we were building up the new people we are in Christ and praying out God's perfect will concerning our future. You, too, are called to:

- Know the new you

- Meditate on the new you

- Hang out with the new you

- Act like the new you

- Talk like the new you

- See the new you

- And pray in the spirit of the new you.

Never forget—if Gideon could change, you can too. If this once fearful, mediocre Benjamite could rise to the occasion of restoring himself and his nation to the best God had to offer in life, so can you. If John could do it, if Paul could do it, if Peter could do it, so can you. They were human new creations just like you who renewed their minds in the presence of God. As He is, so are we in this world. And the Lord is with you, you mighty man or woman of valor!

You can take control of life's situations and walk in the dominion Jesus died to provide.

You can be transformed from glory to glory into the image of Christ's glorious Church.

You can make the great exchange by renewing your mind daily with the mind of Christ in the power of God's Spirit.

God's abundant life can be yours, but you must possess it, you mighty Christian of valor!

Also remember, there are no quick fixes. As you get to know the new you, mediate on the new you, build relationships with the people of God and continually hang out with the new you, act like the new you, speak and look like the new you, pray in the Spirit of the new you and as you make some quality decisions about your physical health and the use of your time, you will be as He is in the earth. And because of you the earth will be blessed!

Chapter 1
[1] Strong, "Greek," entry #2222, p. 35.
[2] Strong, "Greek," entry #4053, p. 57.
[3] Strong, "Greek," entry #1391, p. 24.
[4] Ibid
[5] Hewitt, Eliza E. and Emily D. Wilson.

Chapter 3
[1] Strong, "Greek," entry #1391, p. 24.

Chapter 5
[1] Strong, "Greek," entry #3339, p. 47.

Chapter 6
[1] Strong, "Greek," entry #1097, p. 20.

Chapter 8
[1] Vine, s.v. "truth," Vol. 4, pp. 158-161.

Chapter 10
[1] Strong, "Hebrew," entry #1897, p. 32.

Chapter 15
[1] Briggs, C., F. Brown and S. Driver, s.v. "restraint" #6544, p. 828.

Chapter 24
[1] Strong, "Hebrew," entry #430, p. 12.

Chapter 25
[1] Strong, "Hebrew," entry #3876, p. 59.

REFERENCES

Briggs, C., F. Brown and S. Driver. *The Brown-Driver-Briggs Hebrew and English Lexicon: With an Appendix Containing the Biblical Aramaic.* Massachusetts: Hedrickson Publishers, Incorporated, 1996.

Hewitt, Eliza E. and Emily D. Wilson. "When We All Get to Heaven." *The Hymnal for Worship and Celebration.* Waco: Word Music, 1986.

Strong, James. *Strong's Exhaustive Concordance of the Bible.* "Hebrew and Chaldee Dictionary." "Greek Dictionary of the New Testament." Nashville: Abingdon, 1890.

Vine, W. E. *Expository Dictionary of New Testament Words.* Old Tappan: Fleming H. Revell, 1940.

About the Author

Casey Treat pastors one of the largest churches in the Pacific Northwest—Christian Faith Center—in Seattle, Washington. He is an outstanding minister, author and motivational speaker. Pastor Treat is also the founder of Dominion University in Seattle, serves on the board of directors of Church Growth International—founded by Dr. David Yonggi Cho in Seoul, Korea—and is a co-founding trustee of Oral Roberts' International Charismatic Bible Ministries. His daily television program, *Staying on Course* can be seen on cable and over the air stations daily from coast to coast. His *Success Through Excellence* seminars for business people have motivated many to excel. And his many books and tape series have helped thousands internationally.

Casey and his wife, Wendy, reside in the Seattle area with their three children.

To contact Casey Treat,

write:

Casey Treat

P. O. Box 98800

Seattle, WA 98198

Please include your prayer requests

and comments when you write.

OTHER BOOKS BY CASEY TREAT

Reaching Your Summit

Blueprint for Life

Available from your local bookstore.

Harrison House
Tulsa, Oklahoma 74153

www.harrisonhouse.com

Fast. Easy. Convenient

- ◆ New Book Information
- ◆ Look Inside the Book
- ◆ Press Releases
- ◆ Bestsellers

- ◆ Free E-News
- ◆ Author Biographies
- ◆ Upcoming Books
- ◆ Share Your Testimony

For the latest in book news and author information,
please visit us on the Web at www.harrisonhouse.com.
Get up-to-date zpictures and details on all our powerful and
life-changing products. Sign up for our e-mail newsletter,
Friends of the House, and receive free monthly information
on our authors and products including testimonials, author
announcements, and more!

Harrison House—
Books That Bring Hope, Books That Bring Change

THE HARRISON HOUSE VISION

Proclaiming the truth and the power

Of the Gospel of Jesus Christ

With excellence;

Challenging Christians to

Live victoriously,

Grow spiritually,

Know God intimately.